Anonymous

Origin, Doctrine, Constitution and Discipline of The United Brethren

in Christ

Anonymous

Origin, Doctrine, Constitution and Discipline of The United Brethren in Christ

ISBN/EAN: 9783337030339

Printed in Europe, USA, Canada, Australia, Japan

Cover: Foto ©Thomas Meinert / pixelio.de

More available books at **www.hansebooks.com**

ORIGIN, DOCTRINE,

CONSTITUTION,

AND

DISCIPLINE

OF THE

UNITED BRETHREN IN CHRIST.

———

DAYTON, OHIO:
UNITED BRETHREN PUBLISHING HOUSE,
1889.

CONTENTS.

iv CONTENTS.

DISCIPLINE.

CHAPTER I.

ORIGIN OF THE UNITED BRETHREN IN CHRIST.

In the eighteenth century it pleased the Lord our God to awaken persons in different parts of the world, who should raise up the Christian religion from its fallen state and preach the gospel of Christ crucified in its purity.

About the middle of the said century, the Lord, in mercy, remembered the Germans in America, who, living scattered in this extensive country, seldom had an opportunity to hear the gospel of a crucified Savior preached to them in their native language.

Among others, he raised up WILLIAM OTTERBEIN and MARTIN BOEHM, in the State of Pennsylvania, and GEORGE A. GEETING, in the State of Maryland, armed them with spirit, grace, and strength to labor in his neglected vineyard, and to call, among the Germans in America, sinners to repentance. These men obeyed the call of their Lord and Master. Their labors were blest, and

they established in many places excellent societies and led many precious souls to Jesus Christ.
Their sphere of action spread more and more, so
that they found it necessary to look about for more
fellow-laborers to engage in the vineyard of the
Lord; for the harvest was great and the laborers
few. The Lord called others, who were willing to
devote their strength to his service. Such, then,
were accepted by one or another of the preachers
as fellow-laborers.

The number of members in the society in different parts of the country continued to increase from
time to time, and the gracious work of reformation
spread through the states of Pennsylvania, Mary- ·
land, and Virginia. Several great meetings were
appointed and held annually., On such occasions
OTTERBEIN would hold particular conversations
with the preachers then present, and represent to
them the importance of the ministry and the necessity of their utmost endeavors to save souls. At
one of these meetings it was resolved to hold a
conference with all the preachers, in order to take
into consideration in what manner they might be
most useful.

The first conference was held in the city of Baltimore, Maryland, in the year of our Lord 1789
The following preachers were present :

WM. OTTERBEIN,	ADAM LEHMAN,
MARTIN BOEHM,	JOHN ERNST,
GEO. A. GEETING,	HENRY WEIDNER,

CHRISTIAN NEWCOMER.

The second conference was held in Paradise Township, York County, Pennsylvania, at the house of BRO. SPANGLER, in the year of our Lord 1791. The following preachers were present:

WM. OTTERBEIN, JOHN ERNST,
MARTIN BOEHM, J. G. PFRIMMER,
GEO. A. GEETING, JOHN NEIDIG,
CHRISTIAN NEWCOMER, BENEDICT SANDERS,
ADAM LEHMAN.

After mature deliberation as to how they might labor most usefully in the vineyard of the Lord, they again appointed as fellow-laborers such as they had come to believe had experienced true religion in their souls.

Meantime the number of members continued to increase, and the preachers were obliged to appoint an annual conference, in order to unite themselves more closely and to labor more successfully in the vineyard of the Lord; for some had been Presbyterians or German Reformed, some Lutherans, and others Mennonites. They accordingly appointed a conference to be held on the 25th of September, 1800, in Frederick County, Maryland, at the house of BRO. FREDERICK KEMP. The following preachers were present:

WM. OTTERBEIN, CHRISTIAN KRUM,
MARTIN BOEHM, HENRY KRUM,
GEO. A GEETING, JOHN HERSHEY,
CHRISTIAN NEWCOMER, JACOB GEISINGER,
ADAM LEHMAN, HENRY BOEHM,
ABRAHAM TROKEL, DIETRICK AURAND,
J. G. PFRIMMER.

There they united themselves into a society which bears the name "UNITED BRETHREN IN CHRIST," and elected WM. OTTERBEIN and MARTIN BOEHM as superintendents, or bishops, and agreed that each of them should be at liberty as to the mode and manner of Baptism, to perform it according to his own convictions.

From this time, the society increasing still more and more, preachers were appointed to travel regularly, inasmuch as the number of preaching-places could not otherwise be attended to; and the work spread itself into the states of Ohio and Kentucky. It then became necessary to appoint a conference in the State of Ohio, because it was conceived too laborious for the preachers who labored in those States to travel annually such a great distance to conference.

Meantime BROTHERS BOEHM and GEETING died, and BROTHER OTTERBEIN desired that another bishop should be elected (because infirmity and old age would not permit him to superintend any longer), who should take charge of the society, and preserve discipline and order. It was resolved at a former conference that whenever one of the bishops died another should be elected in his place. Accordingly, BROTHER CHRISTIAN NEWCOMER was elected bishop, to take charge of and superintend the concerns of the society.

The want of a *discipline* in the society had long been deeply felt, and partial attempts to provide one having been made at different times, it was resolved, at the conference held in the State of Ohio, that a general conference should be held in order to accomplish the same, in a manner not derogatory to the word of God. The members of this conference were to be elected from among the preachers in the different parts of the country, by a vote of the society in general. The following brethren were duly elected:

CHRISTIAN NEWCOMER,   DANIEL TROYER,
ABRAHAM HIESTAND,   GEO. BENEDUM,
ANDREW ZELLER,   ABRAHAM TROKEL,
CHRISTIAN BERGER,   HENRY G. SPAYTH,
ABRAHAM MAYER,   I. NISWANDER,
JOHN SCHNEIDER,   CHRISTIAN KRUM,
HENRY KUMLER,   JACOB BOWLUS.

The conference convened on the 6th of June, 1815, near Mount Pleasant, Westmoreland County, Pennsylvania. After mature deliberation, they presented to their brethren a discipline, containing the doctrine and rules of the Church, desiring that they, together with the word of God, should be strictly observed.

God is a God of order, but where there is no order and no church-discipline, the spirit of love and charity will be lost.

Therefore, brethren, we beseech you to follow the example of our Lord, as it is written, "Be kindly affectioned one to another with brotherly love ; in honor preferring one another." Let the mind be in you which was in Christ, who took upon him the form of a servant, humbled himself, and be-

came obedient unto death, even the death of the
cross, that by his grace we may submit ourselves
one to another in the fear of God.   He who will
not submit is in want of humble love.   Jesus said,
"Whosoever of you will be the chiefest shall be
servant of all.   By this shall all men know that ye
are my disciples, if ye have love one to another."
"He that loveth not his brother abideth in death."
Let us walk in newness of life, that the prayer of
our Lord may be answered in us ; that we may be
one in him, and that he may give us the glory
which he gave to his disciples, that we may be
one even as he and the Father are one.   Therefore, beloved brethren, let us strive to be like-
minded, having the same love, being of one accord,
of one mind.   Let no one speak or think evil of
his brother, but pray God that he may grant us his
Spirit, and an earnest desire to lead a truly devoted
life, to the honor and glory of his holy name.
Amen.

———

The foregoing account of the origin of the
CHURCH OF THE UNITED BRETHREN IN CHRIST
appeared in the Discipline of 1815, the first Discipline published.   Only the slightest changes
in phraseology, as the years have passed, have
been made.   The place of the conference of 1800,
probably should be given as at Peter Kemp's,
instead of at Frederick Kemp's, both places being
in the same county.   It is proper to state that
the present Discipline contains the confession

of faith and the constitution as amended according to the action of the General Conference of 1885, and approved and confirmed by the General Conference of 1889. The confession of faith appeared in its first printed form in 1815. The constitution, in its earlier form, was adopted in 1841.

CHAPTER II.

CONFESSION OF FAITH.

In the name of God, we declare and confess before all men the following articles of our belief:

ARTICLE I.

Of God and the Holy Trinity.

We believe in the only true God, the Father, the Son, and the Holy Ghost ; that these three are one— the Father in the Son, the Son in the Father, and the Holy Ghost equal in essence or being with the Father and the Son.

ARTICLE II.

Of Creation and Providence.

We believe that this triune God created the heavens and the earth, and all that in them is, visible and invisible ; that he sustains, protects, and governs these, with gracious regard for the welfare of man, to the glory of his name.

ARTICLE III.

Of Jesus Christ.

We believe in Jesus Christ ; that he is very God and man ; that he became incarnate by the power

of the Holy Ghost and was born of the Virgin
Mary; that he is the Savior and Mediator of the
whole human race, if they with full faith accept
the grace proffered in Jesus; that this Jesus suffered and died on the cross for us, was buried,
rose again on the third day, ascended into heaven,
and sitteth on the right hand of God, to intercede
for us; and that he will come again at the last
day to judge the living and the dead.

ARTICLE IV.
Of the Holy Ghost.

We believe in the Holy Ghost; that he is equal
in being with the Father and the Son; that he
convinces the world of sin, of righteousness, and
of judgment; that he comforts the faithful and
guides them into all truth.

ARTICLE V.
Of the Holy Scriptures.

We believe that the Holy Bible, Old and New
Testaments, is the word of God; that it reveals
the only true way to our salvation; that every true
Christian is bound to acknowledge and receive it
by the help of the Spirit of God as the only rule
and guide in faith and practice.

ARTICLE VI.
Of the Church.

We believe in a holy Christian church, composed of true believers, in which the word of God
is preached by men divinely called, and the ordinances are duly administered; that this divine in-

stitution is for the maintenance of worship, for the edification of believers, and the conversion of the world to Christ.

ARTICLE VII.
Of the Sacraments.

We believe that the sacraments, Baptism, and the Lord's Supper, are to be used in the Church, and should be practiced by all Christians; but the mode of baptism and the manner of observing the Lord's Supper are always to be left to the judgment and understanding of each individual. Also, the baptism of children shall be left to the judgment of believing parents.

The *example* of the washing of feet is to be left to the judgment of each one, to practice or not.

ARTICLE VIII.
Of Depravity.

We believe that man is fallen from original right-eousness, and apart from the grace of our Lord Jesus Christ, is not only entirely destitute of holiness, but is inclined to evil, and only evil, and that continually; and that except a man be born again he cannot see the kingdom of heaven.

ARTICLE IX.
Of Justification.

We believe that penitent sinners are justified before God, only by faith in our Lord Jesus Christ, and not by works ; yet that good works in Christ are acceptable to God, and spring out of a true and living faith.

ARTICLE X.

Of Regeneration and Adoption.

We believe that regeneration is the renewal of the heart of man after the image of God, through the word, by the act of the Holy Ghost, by which the believer receives the spirit of adoption and is enabled to serve God with the will and the affections.

ARTICLE XI.

Of Sanctification.

We believe that sanctification is the work of God's grace, through the word and the Spirit, by which those who have been born again are separated in their acts, words, and thoughts from sin, and are enabled to live unto God, and to follow holiness, without which no man shall see the Lord.

ARTICLE XII.

Of the Christian Sabbath.

We believe that the Christian Sabbath is divinely appointed ; that it is commemorative of our Lord's resurrection from the grave, and is an emblem of our eternal rest ; that it is essential to the welfare of the civil community, and to the permanence and growth of the Christian church, and that it should be reverently observed as a day of holy rest and of social and public worship.

ARTICLE XIII.

Of the Future State.

We believe in the resurrection of the dead ; the future general judgment ; and an eternal state of rewards, in which the righteous dwell in endless life, and the wicked in endless punishment.

CONSTITUTION.

In the name of God, we, the members of the CHURCH OF THE UNITED BRETHREN IN CHRIST, for the work of the ministry, for the edifying of the body of Christ, for the more speedy and effectual spread of the Gospel, and in order to produce and secure uniformity in faith and practice, to define the powers and business of the General Conference as recognized by this church, and to preserve inviolate the popular will of the membership of the Church, do ordain this CONSTITUTION:

ARTICLE I.

SECTION 1. All ecclesiastical power herein granted, to enact or repeal any rule or rules of discipline, is vested in a General Conference, which shall consist of elders and laymen elected in each annual conference district throughout the Church. The number and ratio of elders and laymen, and the mode of their election, shall be determined by the General Conference.

Provided, however, That such elders shall have stood as elders in the conferences which they are

2

to represent for no less time than three years next preceding the meeting of the General Conference to which they are elected ; and that such laymen shall be not less than twenty-five years of age, and shall have been members of the Church six years, and members in the conference districts which they are to represent at least three years next preceding the meeting of the General Conference to which they are elected.

SEC. 2. The General Conference shall convene every four years, and a majority of the whole number of delegates elected shall constitute a quorum.

SEC. 3. The ministerial and lay delegates shall deliberate and vote together as one body; but the General Conference shall have power to provide for a vote by separate orders whenever it deems it best to do so ; and in such cases the concurrent vote of both orders shall be necessary to complete an action.

SEC. 4. The General Conference shall, at each session, elect bishops from among the elders throughout the Church who have stood six years in that capacity.

SEC. 5. The bishops shall be members *ex-officio* and presiding officers of the General Conference; but, in case no bishop be present, the Conference shall choose a president *pro tempore.*

SEC. 6. The General Conference shall determine the number and boundaries of the annual conferences.

SEC. 7. The General Conference shall have power to review the records of the annual conferences and see that the business of each annual conference is done strictly in accordance with the discipline, and approve or annul, as the case may require.

SEC. 8. The General Conference shall have full control of The United Brethren Printing Establishment, The Home, Frontier, and Foreign Missionary Society, The Church-Erection Society, The General Sabbath-school Board, The Board of Education, and Union Biblical Seminary. It shall also have power to establish and manage any other organization or institution within the Church which it may deem helpful in the work of evangelization.

SEC. 9. The General Conference shall have power to establish a court of appeals.

SEC. 10. The General Conference may—two thirds of the members elected thereto concurring—propose changes in, or additions to, the confession of faith ; provided, that the concurrence of three fourths of the annual conferences shall be necessary to their final ratification.

ARTICLE II.

The General Conference shall have power, as provided in Article I, section 1, of this Constitution, to make rules and regulations for the Church; nevertheless, it shall be subject to the following limitations and restrictions:

SECTION 1. The General Conference shall enact no rule or ordinance which will change or destroy the confession of faith, and shall establish no standard of doctrine contrary to the confession of faith.

SEC. 2. The General Conference shall enact no rule which will destroy the itinerant plan.

SEC. 3. The General Conference shall enact no rule which will deprive local preachers of their votes in the annual conferences to which they severally belong.

SEC. 4. The General Conference shall enact no rule which will abolish the right of appeal.

ARTICLE III.

SECTION I. We declare that all secret combinations which infringe upon the rights of those outside their organization, and whose principles and practices are injurious to the Christian character of their members, are contrary to the word of God, and that Christians ought to have no connection with them.

The General Conference shall have power to enact such rules of discipline with respect to such combinations as in its judgment it may deem proper.

SEC. 2. We declare that human slavery is a violation of human rights, and contrary to the word of God. It shall therefore in no wise be tolerated among us.

ARTICLB IV.

The right, title, interest, and claim of all property, both real and personal, of whatever name or description, obtained by purchase or otherwise, by any person or persons, for the use, benefit, and behoof of the Church of the United Brethren in Christ, are hereby fully recognized, and held to vest in the Church aforesaid.

ARTICLE V..

SECTION 1. Amendments to this Constitution may be proposed by any General Conference — two thirds of the members elected thereto concurring — which amendments shall be submitted to a vote of the membership throughout the Church, under regulations authorized by said conference.

A majority of all the votes cast upon any submitted amendment shall be necessary to its final ratification.

SEC. 2. The foregoing amended Constitution shall be in force from and after the first Monday after the second Thursday of May, 1889, upon official proclamation thereof by the Board of Bishops; *provided*, that the General Conference elected for 1889 shall be the lawful legislative body under the amended Constitution, with full power, until its final adjournment, to enact such rules as this amended Constitution authorizes.

CHAPTER IV.

MEMBERS.

SECTION I.

RECEPTION OF MEMBERS.

When at any meeting there are persons who desire to unite with the Church, the preacher present shall call the applicants forward and address them as follows:

DEAR FRIENDS: We greet you as you come seeking admission into the church which our Savior purchased with his own blood, and rejoice with you that through the grace of God you have been brought to a knowledge of the truth, and have been made partakers of his great salvation. The privileges you seek are above price, and the duties enjoined are solemn. It is proper that you publicly confess your faith and avow your purpose by answering the following questions :

Questions to Applicants.

1. Do you believe the Bible to be the word of God, and that therein only is contained the knowledge of the way of salvation ?

2. Have you experienced the pardon of your sins, and have you now peace with God ?

3. Are you determined by the grace of God to follow Christ, renouncing the world and all ungodliness, seeking to lead a life of holiness and devotion to God and his cause?

4. Are you willing to be governed by our church-discipline ?

5. Have you been baptized?

[If the answer be in the negative, then the applicant shall be required to attend to the duty as soon as practicable.]

Acceptance of Applicants.

1. If the persons answer the above questions in the affirmative, and no lawful objections be made

by any member, then the preacher shall give his right hand to such persons as members of our church, and record their names on the church-book ; provided, however, that where a local church deems it advisable for its protection against imposition, a committee may be appointed, who, together with the pastor, may make inquiry as to the advisability of admitting such applicants to membership in the Church according to the foregoing requirements.

Receiving Persons from Other Churches.

When persons come to us with certificates of good standing in other churches, they shall answer the fourth question affirmatively, and the hand of fellowship shall be given them as in other cases.

Seekers.

2. Any persons giving evidence that they are sincerely seeking the Lord, may be received under the watch-care of the Church by having their names placed upon the church-book, but shall not be reported as members, nor shall they have a vote in the Church until they shall have conformed to the rules in the section relating to the reception of members.

3. If any person thus received under the watch-care of the Church shall cease to manifest a desire to seek the Lord, the preacher in charge, by the consent of the local Church or official board, may, at any time, after personal but unsuccessful labor for his salvation, drop the name of such seeker.

Preacher's Responsibility.

4. Any preacher refusing or neglecting to ask the foregoing questions, or who shall receive members into the Church in violation of this order, shall be answerable for the same in the conference of which he is a member.

SECTION II.
DUTIES OF MEMBERS.

1. All members of this church shall acknowledge and confess that they believe the Bible to be the word of God ; that they will henceforth strive, with all their hearts, to seek their eternal welfare in Christ Jesus, and work out their salvation with fear and trembling, to the end that they may be enabled to flee from the wrath to come.

Means of Grace.

2. Every member shall endeavor to lead a godly life ; attend to the ordinances of God's house, namely, baptism and the remembrance of the sufferings and death of our Lord Jesus Christ ; be diligent in prayer, particularly in private, and for his own edification attend, when practicable, all our prayer and class meetings, and meetings for public worship.

Family Piety.

3. Heads of families should never omit to pray with their families, morning and evening, and to set them a good example in all the Christian virtues.

SINGING.

4. We believe it to be the duty of all the people

of God to sing his praises, and to sing them in the great congregation as well as in the private circle. We therefore earnestly recommend to all our people the cultivation of vocal music, so that the singing in our congregations may be improved. As a help to this end, we advise all our people to provide themselves with hymn-books for use in times of public and social worship.

Love to Others.

5. Every one should strive to walk as in the presence of God, and accustom himself to a close communion with God in all his employments ; and never to speak evil of his fellow-beings, but practice love toward friend and foe, do good to the poor, and endeavor to be a follower of Jesus Christ indeed.

Sabbath Observance.

6. Everyone shall keep the Sabbath-day holy, as required in the word of God; neither buy nor sell, but spend the same in exercises of devotion, in reading and hearing the word of God, and in singing spiritual hymns to the honor and glory of God.

Obedience to Government.

7. It is the duty of every member to lead a quiet, peaceable, and godly life among men, as it becomes a Christian to live in peace, and be subject to the higher or ruling powers, as the word of God requires.

Sabbath-School.

8. It is the duty of all our members to encour-

age our Sabbath-schools by their presence when practicable, and always to give them their aid and influence. ·

Support of the Gospel.

9. It is the duty of all members of the Church to pay toward the support of the itinerant ministry, quarterly, or oftener if need be, in proportion to their ability, as God has prospered them ; for the Lord hath ordained that they who preach the gospel shall live of the gospel, (I Cor. 9: 14 ; I. Tim, 5: 18.), and we do earnestly recommend to all of our people the Bible method of weekly contributions. "Upon the first day of the week let every one of you lay by him in store, as God hath prospered him." I. Cor. 16:2.

Support of General Interests.

10. It is also the duty of all our members to contribute, according to their ability, to the support of the various benevolent interests of the Church.

Receiving the Pastor.

11. It is the duty of all districts, stations, circuits, and missions to cheerfully receive the preachers appointed by the stationing committee of the respective annual conferences.

Care of the Poor.

12. Each member of our church should willingly and freely contribute quarterly, or oftener if need be, as God has prospered him (I. Cor. 16: 2), to the support of the helpless poor.   ＼

When it is known by any of our class-leaders
that there are poor members among them, who
by sickness, accident, or other unavoidable circumstances, have been brought to want, it shall be
the duty of the leader in charge to wait upon the
class, or to appoint some one to do so, to ask alms,
money, clothing, or produce, as the circumstances
may require. Should any one class be too poor
to relieve its poor, it shall then be made known
to the pastor, whose duty it shall be to inform
the different classes on his charge; and f it sho uld
so happen that any one charge should be insufficient to meet the wants of the poor, it shall be the
duty of the presiding elder to present the matter
on the different charges at their quarterly conferences, so that the unavoidably poor of our church
may be considered and provided for. (I. John 3:
17; Psalm 12: 1, 2.)

Non-conformity to the World.

13. Inasmuch as the Lord has commanded us
not to be conformed to this world (Rom. 12: 2), to
lay apart all filthiness, and superfluity of naughti-
ness (James 1: 21), and as the principles of the
Christian religion, as taught by both the precepts
and the example of the meek and adorable Savior,
are in strict and perfect accordance with these
commandments, we therefore humbly beseech and
admonish the members of our church to observe
these divine precepts. " In like manner also, that
women adorn themselves in modest apparel, with
shamefacedness and sobriety ; not with braided

hair, or gold, or pearls, or costly array; but (which becometh women professing godliness) with good works" (1. Tim. 2: 9, 10); and "whose adorning let it not be that outward adorning of plaiting the hair, and of wearing of gold, or of putting on of apparel ; but let it be the hidden man of the heart, in that which is not corruptible, even the ornament of a meek and quiet spirit, which is in the sight of God of great price." (1. Peter 3: 3, 4.)

NECESSITY OF UNION AMONG OURSELVES.

14. Let us be deeply sensible (from what we have known) of the evil of a division in principle, spirit, or practice, and of the dreadful consequences to ourselves and others. If we are united, what can stand before us? If we are divided, we shall injure ourselves, the work of God, and the souls of our people. To this end :

1. Let us be deeply convinced of the absolute necessity of union.

2. Let us pray earnestly for one another, and speak truly and freely to one another.

3. When we meet, let us never part without prayer, if prayer is at all practicable.

4. Let us take great care not to despise one another's gifts.

5. Let us never speak lightly of one another.

6. Let us defend one another's character in everything, so far as is consistent with truth.

7. Let us labor in honor, each preferring another before himself.

8. We recommend a serious examination of the

causes, evils, and cures of heart and church divisions.

Duty of Obedience.

15. The foregoing rules are drawn up for the better regulation of our church ; and we believe they are founded in the word of God, and incumbent on all who are members of our church to observe. Should any violate or habitually neglect these rules, they shall be, by their respective class leaders, admonished to reformation ; and should they not reform, they shall be suspended or expelled, as the case may require, by vote of the local church or official board.

SECTION III.
TRIAL OF MEMBERS.

When members trespass against one another, let the following directions be followed: .

" If thy brother shall trespass against thee, go and tell him his fault between thee and him alone: if he shall hear thee, thou hast gained thy brother. But if he will not hear thee, then take with thee one or two more. And if he shall neglect to hear them, tell it unto the church: but if he neglect to hear the church, let him be unto thee as a heathen man and a publican ;" that is, he shall be expelled by the local church or official board.

Immoral Conduct.

In case of members accused of immoral conduct, the class or official board shall appoint one or more to visit the accused person, and, if possible, reclaim him ; but if unsuccessful, and the guilt be denied, he shall be tried by the class to which he belongs, or a committee thereof, chosen by the parties concerned, with the preacher in charge of the circuit or station, who shall be chairman ; and if found guilty, the accused shall be expelled, by a vote of the local church or official board, unless satisfaction be given. If the accused refuse to choose his committee-man when properly notified, the quarterly conference shall choose a second person, and these two a third, which committee shall try the case and decide. Yet cases may happen where it would be expedient to choose a committee from some other class or classes than the one to which the parties belong, in which case it shall be lawful to do so. Also, an elder may be chosen as chairman, should the preacher in charge deem it best to do so. Should any member be dissatisfied with the decision, an appeal may be had to the quarterly conference, by giving notice thereof to the preacher in charge, or secretary of the trial. (See section on appeals). In such case, however, the same persons shall not sit in judgment on the same case.

Disobedience to the Order of the Church.

In cases of neglect of duty of any kind, imprudent conduct, indulging in sinful tempers or words, or disobedience to the order and discipline of the Church: First, let private reproof be given by the preacher or leader; and if there be an acknowledgment of the fault, proper humiliation, and a promise to reform, the person may be borne with.

On a second offense, the preacher or leader shall take with him one or two faithful members. On a third offense, let the case be brought before the local church, or class, or a select committee; and if there be no satisfactory humiliation, the offender shall be expelled by vote of the local church or official board. In case the accused shall deny his guilt and demand a trial, and there be a reasonable doubt or question about his guilt, he shall be tried by a committee, and if found guilty, he shall be expelled. In case of trial under this clause, the leader shall act in behalf of the local church; or if the leader be the offender, the steward shall act as prosecutor.

Disputes.

In case of a dispute between members or preachers, the preacher to whom it shall be known shall inquire into the circumstances of the case, and, if necessary, shall recommend to the contending parties a reference to a committee, consisting of one arbiter chosen by the plaintiff, and another by the defendant, and a third by these two; then these three are to decide. But if the preacher to whom the dispute is known shall refuse or neglect to act, then the quarterly conference shall appoint one to carry out the rule; and if either or both disputants refuse to choose an arbiter, the quarterly conference shall appoint the first and second, and these two a third, who shall hear the case and decide.

Right of Appeal.

Should either party be dissatisfied with the de-

cision, such may have a right to an appeal to the
next quarterly conference for a second arbitration,
where each party shall choose two arbiters, and
the four shall choose a fifth, a decision of a majority of whom shall be final.   Any person refusing to abide by this decision shall be expelled
without further trial.

Going to Law Forbidden.

Every member refusing, in case of debt or dispute, to refer the matter to arbitration when recommended to him by a preacher or leader, or who
shall enter into a lawsuit with another member
before these measures are taken, shall be expelled
without further process, and his name be so recorded upon the church-record by the preacher in
charge, or the class-leader, except when the case
is of such a nature as to require and justify a process at law, as executors or administrators, or
when a member is in danger of suffering an unex-
pected loss of property.

Record of Trials.

Every class-leader shall keep a record of the
proceedings of church-trials, deaths, expulsions,
and removals, in a book provided for that purpose;
and it shall be his duty, in case of an appeal, to
furnish his record to the quarterly conference.

Order in Trials.

All church-trials shall be conducted in a consistent Christian manner, without the employment of
magistrates and attorneys to administer oaths and
conduct investigations.

SECTION IV.

TRANSFER AND DISMISSAL OF MEMBERS.

Transfers.

When members of our church move from one field to another, they shall obtain a certificate of transfer by a vote of the majority of the class to which they belong, signed by a preacher or leader, except where they are not in reach of a class ; in which case any of our preachers may give a certificate to such persons if they are known to be in good standing ; and the pastor shall notify the preacher in charge nearest the point to which the member moves.

Amenability of Certified Members.

Any person receiving a certificate of membership of good standing, is amenable to the class from which he receives it, until he deposit his certificate with some other local church.

Limit of Certificate.

A member who receives a certificate is required to present it to some class, or return it to the class by which it was issued, within eighteen months, provided that the holder of the certificate is within reach of a local church ; otherwise it shall become null and void.

Dismissal.

If any of our members desire to leave the Church, and their Christian life has been good, and they have settled all of their subscriptions and assessments, they shall receive an honorable dismissal

3

from the Church by a vote of the local church, signed by the pastor.

Membership of Preachers.

An annual-conference member may be received into a class on his ministerial credentials, so long as said credentials are held in force by the conference to which he is amenable.

CHAPTER V.

GOVERNMENT OF THE CHURCH.

SECTION I.

CLASSES.

Election of Leader.

1. A class shall consist of three or more members, who shall annually elect one member from their own or some other class, to be called their leader; except that in the organization of children's classes the pastor shall appoint a leader. This election shall be held immediately preceding the annual conference.

Division of Classes.

2. Classes shall be divided by a committee, consisting of the preacher in charge and one or more brethren, elected by the local church at any place where it may be deemed necessary.

Disbanding Classes.

3. In case it becomes impracticable to keep up an organization, the members at such place shall be required to join the nearest class within six

months; and anyone failing to do so may be dropped.

SECTION II.

CLASS-LEADERS.

Qualifications.

1. It shall be the leader's duty to lead a pious life and set a godly example before his class; carefully to study the Holy Scriptures, fully qualifying himself for the faithful performance of his duties as leader and counselor of his class.

Holding Meetings.

2. It shall be his duty to meet his class, in class or prayer-meeting, as often as practicable, to speak to them concerning their spiritual welfare, and exhort them to unity and love. He shall extend the freedom of our prayer and class-meetings to all sincere and well-disposed persons who may desire to attend them.

Visiting the Sick and Delinquent.

3. When any of his members are sick, or delinquent in the performance of any of their duties as Christians, he shall visit them, pray or otherwise labor with them, as circumstances may require.

Dismissal for Delinquency.

Any class-leader failing to discharge these duties may, on complaint, be removed by the quarterly conference.

SECTION III.

CLASS-STEWARDS.

Every class shall have one or more stewards,

who shall annually be appointed by the preacher
in charge, subject to the approval of the class.

Collections for Pastors.

1. The steward shall collect quarterly contributions, or oftener than quarterly, if needed, for
the support of traveling preachers. He shall keep
an accurate account of the amount paid by each
member of the class, in a book provided for that
purpose, and report the same, with name and
amount, to each quarterly conference or official
meeting.

Elements for the Lord's Supper.

2. It shall also be his duty to provide the ele-
ments for the sacrament of the Lord's Supper,
always securing unfermented wine.

Dismissal for Delinquency.

3. For the faithful discharge of his duties as
steward, he shall be accountable to the quarterly
conference, which shall have power to dismiss him
for official delinquency.

SECTION IV.
OFFICIAL MEETINGS FOR STATIONS.
Members.

1. The members of the official meeting shall be
the properly recognized members of the quarterly
conference.

2. The preacher in charge shall be the president
of the meeting; and in his absence one of the
members shall be elected president *pro tem.*

3. The president shall call the meeting to order,
and begin and conclude with prayer.

Duties of Official Meetings.

1. It shall be the duty of the official meeting to elect a secretary, who shall make a record of the proceedings of the meeting.

2. To elect a treasurer, whose duty it shall be to receive from stewards all moneys that have been collected, and receipt therefor; and said treasurer shall pay out all moneys in his hands as the official meeting may direct.

3. To receive a statement from each class-leader in reference to the prosperity of religion in his class.

4. This body shall meet once a month, and may meet oftener if circumstances require.

5. It shall be the duty of the official meeting to receive all reports of subscriptions, and moneys collected and disbursed for the interest of the station; and all persons intrusted with subscriptions or moneys shall report the same to the meeting as soon as possible.

6. It shall be the duty of the official meeting to submit its acts to the quarterly conference for examination and approval.

Section V.
QUARTERLY CONFERENCE.

Members.

The members of the quarterly conference shall be the presiding elder of the district, the preacher in charge, and all the properly-recognized preachers, exhorters, leaders, stewards, church treasurers, and trustees of meeting and parsonage houses, and superintendents of Sabbath-schools (when said trustees and superintendents are members of the Church of the United Brethren in Christ), who reside within the bounds of the circuit, station, or mission, or hold membership therein, Such members as are present at any regular meeting shall constitute a quorum for the transaction of business. It shall be the duty of the quarterly conference to open and close with prayer.

Duties of the Quarterly Conference.

1. In the absence of the presiding elder, the quarterly conference shall elect a chairman *pro tem.*, whose official acts shall be valid.

2. It shall elect a secretary, whose duty it shall be to keep a correct record of all their proceedings in a book provided for that purpose, in which the names of all the members composing the said conference shall be entered.

3. It shall make inquiry into the moral deportment and official character of all its members.

4. In stations it shall elect at the last quarterly conference of the year a church treasurer, wherever desirable, who shall be a member of the quarterly conference.

5. It shall enforce discipline in all the classes under its jurisdiction, but in no case disorganize a class unless the preliminary steps have been taken as required in Chapter V., Section I., of Discipline.

6. It shall make settlement with the stewards and traveling preachers.

Appeals and Trials.

7. It shall receive and try all appeals, references, and complaints that may come regularly before it ; but no member of quarterly conference can be suspended or expelled from the Church prior to a committee trial. When a quarterly-conference preacher or exhorter is accused of any misdemeanor, he shall be tried by a committee of three, of which the accused shall choose one and the quarterly conference a second, and these two a third. If the accused refuse or neglect to choose his committee-man after being properly notified, the quarterly conference shall choose a first and a second person, and these two a third, who shall hear the case and decide; and if the accused is found guilty he shall be silenced ; provided, however, that either party shall have the right of appeal to the next quarterly conference for a new trial.

Licensing of Preachers.

8. It shall grant license to exhort or preach to such as may have been recommended by at least two thirds of the class of which they are members; provided, however, that none shall receive license who cannot give satisfactory evidence of their call, religious experience, soundness in doctrine, and ttachment to our church and government. All applicants for quarterly-conference license to preach shall be examined by quarterly conference according to Chapter VI., Section II., of Discipline.

9. It shall renew the license of exhorters and

quarterly-conference licensed preachers annually, if they are found worthy, and to arrange a plan for the local preachers to preach regularly at stated places, as the quarterly conference may direct.

Recommending to the Annual Conference.

10. After such licentiate preachers have stood in that capacity one or more years, and have completed the course of reading required by Discipline, the quarterly conference may recommend them to the annual conference.

Permanent License.

11. Quarterly-conference preachers having passed the course of reading required by Discipline, may be granted a permanent license, not subject to annual renewal.

Excusing from Examination.

12. The quarterly conference may excuse from the course of reading a local preacher who has attained the age of fifty years.

Class Connection.

13. All exhorters and quarterly and annual conference preachers are required to join some convenient class, and upon neglect or refusal to do so shall lose their official relation.

General Steward.

14. The quarterly conference, at its last session in each year, shall appoint a steward for the charge, whose duty it shall be to assist the class-stewards in securing the preacher's salary, and receive and audit the stewards' reports.

Estimating Committee.

15. The quarterly conference shall, at its last session for the year, appoint an estimating committee, which committee shall meet at the time and place specified by the preacher appointed to the charge for the ensuing year, and make out an estimate of the regular expenses of the circuit, station, or mission, and apportion the same among the different appointments according to their several abilities, and report the same to the quarterly conference for ratification.

Apportionment to the Classes.

16. Each class, after receiving its apportionment, shall, as soon as convenient, on the call of the leader or steward, hold a meeting and appoint a committee whose duty it shall be to make a distribution of the apportionment to the members severally according to their ability, to be paid quarterly or monthly; provided, however, that it shall be the privilege of any class to collect the amount apportioned to it by subscription or otherwise.

Questions.

1. Where shall our next quarterly conference be held?
2. Is there anything more to be done?

Appeals.

Any exhorter or preacher dissatisfied with the decision of a quarterly conference shall, within thirty days after the quarterly conference, notify the secretary, in writing, of his intention to appeal, together with his reasons for so doing; and it shall be the duty of the secretary to take or send a certified copy of the proceedings, the notification, and reasons assigned, to the annual conference.

In all cases of appeal, whether to the quarterly or annual conference, or to the Court of Appeals, the course laid down in the section on appeals is the proper course to be pursued.

SECTION VI.
ANNUAL CONFERENCE.
Members.

1. The annual conference shall consist of all the elders and licentiate preachers who have been duly received by the conference, and one layman from each charge in the conference, who shall be elected by the quarterly conference, at the third or last session in the year. The laymen thus chosen shall have all the privileges and rights of ministers in the annual conference, except the right to vote upon the reception or expulsion of preachers, and the passing of preachers in the course of reading.

Devotions.

2. A portion of scripture shall be read at the opening of the session ; also, there shall be singing and prayer each day, at the opening and closing of conference.

Secretaries.

3. The conference shall elect one or more secretaries, as the case may require, who, in addition to discharging the regular duties of secretary, shall, immediately on the adjournment of the annual

conference, transmit to the publishing agent at
Dayton, Ohio, a true transcript of the footings of
the conference chart.

Bishop Pro Tem.

4. If no bishop should be present, it shall be
the duty of the annual conference to elect a bishop
pro tem., whose official acts shall be valid.

Examinations.

5. All preachers shall report in person or by
letter, and be examined respecting their deportment toward their fellow-beings, whether their
conduct in life be blameless, and whether they
employ as much time as practicable to promote
the kingdom of God, (according to Titus, 1st chapter, 7th to 9th verse, and II. Tim., 2d chapter, 15th
verse,) and if found delinquent they shall be admonished or advised, as the case may require. But
should all admonition or advice fail, then the name
of the delinquent person shall be erased from the
roll of the conference.

Absentees.

6. Should any member of the annual conference
absent himself from the session of conference three
years in succession, without giving a satisfactory
reason for so doing, his name may be erased from
the roll of the conference.

Electioneering Forbidden.

7. No preacher shall be permitted to electioneer
favorably to his own election to any office or dele-
gation in the Church ; and should anyone be found

doing so, he shall be accountable to the next annual conference of which he is a member, to be dealt with according to the judgment of said conference.

Authority of the Annual Conference.

8. An annual conference may adopt rules for its own government, not in conflict with the Discipline of the Church.

Questions.

9. The following questions shall also be asked by the presiding officer:

1. Have any of the preachers died during the last year?
2. Who are candidates for the ministry?
3. Are any to be ordained to the office of elder?
4. What has been collected for contingent expenses and the salary of traveling preachers?
5. What has been done for missions?
6. What has been done for Sabbath-schools?
7. Has reckoning been made with the traveling preachers?
8. Who are the presiding elders?
9. Where are the preachers stationed this year?
10. Where shall our next conference be held?
11. Is there anything else to be done?
12. Is all that has been done entered upon record?

SECTION VII.
GENERAL CONFERENCE.
Members.

(See Constitution.)

Conference Representation.

The annual conferences shall be represented in the General Conference according to the following ratios :

Not less than three nor more than six from each annual conference distriƈt. All conferences having less than three thousand members shall be entitled to two elders and one layman. All conferences having three thousand and under six thousand five hundred members, shall be entitled to three elders and one layman. All conferences having six thousand five hundred members and over that number, shall be entitled to four elders and two laymen.

Bishops' Announcement.

The Board of Bishops shall as early as possible announce the number of delegates to which each conference shall be entitled, as appears from the statistics of the annual conferences at the end of the third year of the term.

Eleƈtion of Delegates.

1. It shall be the duty ot each annual conference to appoint a committee of three, and three alternates. ıɷ ɹeceive and publicly count the votes, and issue certıficates oɩ eleƈtion to those receiving the highest numbeɩ ot votes, also to furnish each preacheɩ in charge with a list of the names of all the eligible elders and of all the eligible laymen nominated. It shall be the duty of the lay representatives in each annual conference during the

annual session next preceding the election, to nominate by ballot three times the number of laymen to be elected. This shall not be construed as depriving any member of the right to vote for other laymen eligible, if desirous of doing so.

2. The leaders and stewards of each class shall constitute a board of election, who shall be furnished a copy of the above-named list, by the preacher in charge, at least ten months before the sitting of the General Conference; and the election shall be held invariably in the month of November next preceding the sitting of said conference.

3. It shall be the duty of each board of election to appoint a meeting of the members of their respective classes or churches, as the case may be, for the purpose of electing, by ballot, their dele. gates to represent them in General Conference.

Absent Voters.

4. Should any member be incapacitated by age or affliction to attend such meetings, and should any minister be absent on his charge, they may send their ballots containing the names of their choice, with their own names signed on the back of their ballots; provided, no votes shall be counted except those cast on the day appointed for said meeting.

Election Returns.

5. It shall be the duty of each board of election invariably to sign, inclose, and seal each bill of election, and keep a correct copy of the same, also a list of the names of all members voting, and im-

mediately transmit a copy of such bill, stating what
class, circuit, mission, or station, to the committee
appointed by the annual conference.

Publication of Elections.

6. Said committee shall make out a list of all
the persons voted for, and of the number of votes
for each; and should any two or more of the candidates have an equal number of votes, the committee shall determine, by lot, which of them is
elected. They shall also forward by the first of
February the names of those elected to the conference Printing Establishment for publication. They
shall also transmit to the publishing agent at Dayton, Ohio, a complete list of all persons voted for,
and the number of votes cast for each, which
record shall be furnished the ensuing General
Conference, and if one or more of those elected
should be prevented by death, sickness, or otherwise from attending, it shall be the duty of the
tellers or the secretary of the General Conference
to notify the next highest on the bill to take his
place, and so descend, if need be, to the last candidate. No bills of election received by the tellers
after the first of January shall be counted.

Bills of Election.

7. It shall be the duty of each presiding elder
to furnish each preacher in charge on his district
with blank bills of election, which shall be distrib-
uted by the preachers to their respective boards
of election.

Delegates' Expenses.

The annual conference next preceding the election of delegates to the General Conference shall ascertain the amount of money that will be necessary to defray the expenses of its delegates to General Conference, and apportion the same among its different fields of labor.; and the preacher in charge shall collect and forward such amount to the presiding elder of his district, who shall transmit the amount to the tellers by the first of February preceding the General Conference. Should any preacher neglect his duty, he shall be accountable therefor to the next annual conference.

Examination of Annual Conferences.

It shall be the duty of the General Conference to examine the administration of each annual conference, whether it has strictly observed the rules, and preserved the *moral* and *doctrinal* principles of the Discipline in all its transactions.

Election of Officers.

In the election of all officers of the General Conference, a majority of all the votes shall be necessary to a choice.

CHAPTER VI.

MINISTRY OF THE CHURCH.

SECTION I.

EXHORTERS.

How Licensed.

Any person wishing to obtain license to exhort must obtain from the class of which he is a member, by a vote of two thirds of the members, a recommendation in writing, signed by the leader, or preacher in charge, to the quarterly conference of the circuit, station, or mission to which he belongs, which may license him, subject to an examination on questions for applicants for quarterly-conference license to preach.

Exhorters' Duties.

Exhorters shall make appointments wherever acceptable to the people; read portions of sacred scripture, exhorting therefrom; exhorting saints, that they with purpose of heart should cleave to the Lord, and sinners to flee from the wrath to come; and this they shall do as often as practicable.

Renewal of License.

The license of an exhorter is subject to renewal annually, at the discretion of the quarterly conference.

SECTION II.

QUARTERLY-CONFERENCE PREACHERS.

How Licensed.

Any person wishing to obtain license to preach, must obtain from the class of which he is a member, by a vote of two thirds of the members, a recommendation in writing, signed by the leader or preacher, to the quarterly conference of the circuit, station, or mission to which he belongs; *provided*, that the person making application shall be examined by the quarterly conference, and the following questions asked by the chairman.

Examination of Applicants.

1. Do you believe our confession of faith as set forth in our book of Discipline?

2. Have you now peace with God through our Lord Jesus Christ?

3. What is your motive in desiring permission to preach the gospel?

4. Are you satisfied with our church-government?

5. Will you submit yourself to the counsel of your brethren?

6. What is your knowledge of depravity, of redemption, of faith, of repentance, of justification, and of sanctification?

7. Will you abstain from the use of tobacco?

It shall be the privilege of the chairman to ask any other question or questions that he may deem necessary.

A man divorced from his wife, except on scriptural and legal grounds, shall not be granted license.

Course of Reading.

Quarterly-conference licensed preachers are required to pursue the course of reading prescribed in our book of Discipline, and to be examined annually by the presiding elder and preacher in charge at the fourth quarterly meeting.

Renewal of License.

The license of a quarterly-conference preacher who is not otherwise exempted by reason of passing the prescribed course of study, is subject to

renewal annually, at the discretion of the quarterly
conference.

Recommendation to Annual Conference.

After such licentiate preachers have stood in that
capacity one or more years, the quarterly conference may recommend them to the annual conference.

All preachers recommended to the annual conference, and not received, shall sustain their former
relation.

SECTION III.

ANNUAL-CONFERENCE PREACHERS.

How Received.

Every person proposed as a preacher shall be
examined by the annual conference or a select
committee thereof; and the following questions
shall be asked him:

Preacher's Examination.

1.   Have you known God in Christ Jesus to be a
sin-pardoning God?

2.   Have you now peace with God; and is the
love of God shed abroad in your heart by the Holy
Spirit?

3.   Do you believe the Bible to be the word of
God, and that therein is contained the only true
way to our salvation?

4.   What foundation have you for such belief?

5.   Do you follow after holiness?

6.   What is your motive for desiring permission
to preach the gospel?

7. Do you believe that man, apart from the grace of our Lord Jesus Christ, is fallen from original righteousness, and is not only entirely destitute of holiness, but is inclined to evil, and only evil, and that continually; and that except a man be born again he cannot see the kingdom of heaven?

8. What is your knowledge of redemption, of faith, of repentance, justification, and sanctification?

9. Does your own salvation, and the salvation of your fellow-mortals, lie nearer to your heart than all other things in the world?

10. Will you subject yourself to the counsel of your brethren in the Lord?

11. Are you satisfied with our church-government?

12. Are you willing, as much as is in your power, to assist in upholding our itinerant plan?

13. Will you abstain from the use of tobacco?

Licensing Women.

Not wishing to hinder any Christian, who may be moved by the Holy Spirit, to labor in the vineyard of the Lord for the salvation of souls, it is ordered that whenever any godly woman presents herself before the quarterly or annual conference as an applicant for authority to preach the gospel among us, she may be granted license, provided she complies with the usual conditions required of men who wish to enter the ministry of our church. When such person shall have passed the required examination before the regular committees, she may, after the usual probation, be ordained.

Qualifications of Applicants.

None can be admitted without having a recommendation from the quarterly conference, and then only to be received on probation ; but if the conference should, on examination, find that the candidate's abilities are insufficient to preach the gospel, it may refer him back to the quarterly conference for further instruction.

A man divorced from his wife, except on scriptural and legal grounds, shall not be granted license.

An Expelled Preacher.

When a preacher or elder has been expelled or formally withdraws from one annual conference, he shall not be received into another without the consent of the conference with which he was formerly connected.

Preacher's Transfer.

1. A preacher or elder who shall labor in the bounds of an annual conference, other than the one to which he belongs, for two years, shall be required to obtain a transfer from the conference to which he belongs and to unite with the conference in whose bounds he labors, or to return to his own conference for work; provided, that presidents and professors of schools and colleges, and others engaged in general church-work, shall be exempt from this requirement.

2. A preacher removing from one conference to

another shall, when he applies to the latter for admission, produce a transfer from the conference to which he formerly belonged, signed by the presiding officer, or published in the minutes of the conference from which he has been transferred.

Limit of Transfer.

A preacher or elder who receives a transfer is required to present said transfer to another conference, or to return it to the conference by which it was issued within two years after its date. Otherwise the transfer shall be null and void, and the name of the preacher shall be published as no longer connected with our church as a minister.

Accountability of Transferred Preachers.

A preacher or elder receiving a transfer shall be a member of the quarterly conference in whose bounds he may reside, and also be accountable for his moral and official conduct to the annual conference granting said transfer, until his transfer be received by the conference to which he has been transferred.

SECTION IV.
RECEPTION OF PREACHERS FROM OTHER CHURCHES.

When preachers from other churches come to us with certificates of good standing in the church in which they have held membership; or with transfers from a conference, presbytery, or synod, and give satisfaction to the annual conference concerning their agreement on the doctrine, discipline, government, and usages of our church, the conference may receive them. If they be ordained elders they must pass the examination required of candidates for elders' orders, but they may be exempt from the laying on of hands.

SECTION V.
CLASSIFICATION OF THE MINISTRY.

The ministry of the Church shall be classified after the following order: Itinerants, superannuated, supernumerary, and local.

Itinerants.

To this class shall belong all annual-conference ministers; provided, however, that they have passed the probation of three years in the annual conference, and have been, during this time, and are still engaged in the regular work of the Church.

Superannuated.

To this class shall belong such itinerants as are from age or physical infirmities unable to pursue the regular work of the ministry.

Supernumerary.

To this class shall belong such as have been admitted to the itineracy and are willing to work, but for whom the conferences and Church, for the time being, are not able to find work, or who, by their own request, have been voted to such relation.

Local.

To this class shall belong such annual-conference preachers as are not admitted to the itineracy.

Class—How Determined.

The annual conference shall determine to which of the foregoing classes each minister shall belong. Should an itinerant leave in an irregular way the work assigned him, he shall forfeit his standing as an itinerant.

Evangelists.

Persons engaged in evangelistic work shall not be encouraged by our ministers if such evangelists do not hold membership in quarterly or annual conference.

SECTION VI.

ELDERS.

Elders' Probation.

After a probation of three years, a preacher may be presented to the annual conference for elders' orders; whereupon the bishop shall propose to the conference the following questions:

Questions Regarding a Candidate.

1. Is he blameless touching the marriage state?
2. Is his deportment in the social circle marked with watchful sobriety?
3. Is he hospitable toward the afflicted and needy?
4. Is he faithful in the public ministration of God's word, and diligent in reading and study?
5. Is his household subject to rules of piety?

Should the above questions be answered in the affirmative, a committee of three or five elders shall be appointed, before whom the candidate shall appear, and answer to the following questions; namely,

Committee Examination.

1. Upon what foundation do you believe the Bible to be the word of God?
2. How do you prove the fall of man by transgression?
3. How do you prove the redemption of man by Jesus Christ?
4. Do you believe in the godhead of Jesus Christ?
5. What foundation have you for such a belief?
6. Do you believe in the Holy Ghost as presented in our confession of faith?
7. Upon what evidence do you believe this?
8. Do you believe in future everlasting punishment?

Duties of the Committee.

It shall be the privilege of the committee, in the close, to propose any question touching the answers given, wherein their understanding may not have been distinct. It shall also be their duty to make out, sign, and deliver to conference a report of each case which may have been before them.

Election to Elders' Orders.

If the committee and conference find the candidate worthy, by a majority of the votes of the elders of conference he may be elected to ordination.

Limit of Probation.

When circumstances demand it, a licentiate may be presented to conference for ordination at any time prior to a probation of three years, provided two thirds of the elders present vote for the same.

Duties of Elders.

It is the duty of an elder to preach the gospel, to baptize, to administer the Lord's Supper, to solemnize marriages, to perform all parts of divine service, to be an example to the flock of Christ by imitating His moral example; and in a very special manner it shall be the duty of an elder to cherish and encourage young ministers, and always to be looking for those whom God has called to preach, and advise them to take up the cross, and begin the work without delay, that the labor of the gospel harvest may be faithfully performed.

SECTION VII.

PRESIDING ELDERS.

Election of Presiding Elders.

Presiding elders shall be elected by annual conference by ballot. A majority of the whole number of votes shall be necessary to a choice.

Support of Presiding Elders.

It shall be the duty of each annual conference to make such regulations for the support of the presiding elders as they in their wisdom may think best calculated to accomplish the desired end.

Stationing Presiding Elders.

Presiding elders shall be stationed by the bishop and two elders or preachers from each presiding-elder district.

Duties of Presiding Elders.

1. The duties of a presiding elder are to travel through the district appointed him, and to preach as often as practicable.

2. He shall appoint the quarterly and camp meetings, and attend them. He shall hold quarterly conferences, and administer the ordinances of God's house. He shall inquire whether the preachers do their duty, and exhort them to maintain discipline and order, love and seriousness in the Church. He may also call extra sessions by the consent of a majority of the quarterly conference members.

3. It shall be his duty to make strict inquiry whether each itinerant minister has received the amount of salary due him, and in case of a deficiency, to make an earnest effort to secure the balance due.

4. Each presiding elder shall make a report in writing, of his district, annually, to the annual conference.

Power to Exchange Preachers.

The presiding elder may, in conjunction with two elders, preachers, exhorters, or leaders (one from each circuit), change the preachers in his district.

Vacancy Filled by Appointment.

Should any district, through death, resignation, or otherwise, be without a presiding elder, information shall be immediately given to the bishop, who shall appoint an elder to preside in said district until the ensuing annual conference.

SECTION VIII.
BISHOPS.

Election of Bishops.

The General Conference shall elect bishops for the term of four years, by a majority of the whole number of votes, to be, at the option of conference, re-elected. The bishops must be capable of attending the conferences assigned them; otherwise they cannot be elected; *provided, however,* that the General Conference may elect a bishop *emeritus* when it deems it proper to do so; *provided further,* such bishop has served the Church in the episcopal office forty years consecutively.

Stationing of Bishops.

Bishops shall be assigned their districts by the General Conference; and in the fields thus assigned them they shall devote their whole time. They shall be required to reside within the bounds of the district assigned them, if practicable; *provided, however,* that they shall have the privilege of making such temporary interchanges as the welfare of their districts may demand.

The four bishops east of the Rocky Mountains shall arrange the times of holding the several conferences, and attend them in rotation as far as possible.

Salaries of Bishops.

The General Conference shall fix the salaries of the bishops and specify the amounts to be raised for their moving and traveling expenses and house rent. Apportionments to meet these salaries and expenses shall be made to the Church by the bishops. Apportionments thus made to annual conferences and mission districts shall be assessed by the various fields of labor according to the ability of each.

DUTIES OF BISHOPS.

Presiding at Conferences.

1. It is the duty of bishops to preside over the annual and general conferences, and strictly examine into the moral and official character of the members of the annual conferences in the bounds of their districts, and insist upon it that all the laws of the Church are faithfully executed.

Stationing the Preachers.

2. In conjunction with the presiding elders of the past and present year they may fix the appointments of the traveling preachers for the several circuits, stations, and missions; provided, however, that where there is but one presiding elder on the committee, the conference may elect to the same another elder from the elders not asking for work from said committee.

Stationing the Presiding Elders.

3. The bishop, in conjunction with two elders, elected by ballot, from each presiding-elder district, shall appoint the presiding elders to their respective districts.

Ordination of Preachers.

4. It shall be their duty to perform the rite of ordination at the annual conferences, and at such other times and places as circumstances may require, but only upon such persons as have passed the usual examination required of candidates for ordination, by a committee of three elders chosen for that purpose by one of the bishops.

Annual Meeting.

5. The bishops shall hold annual meetings, in which they shall determine the time of holding the annual conferences, determine the order of the holding of the conferences, and who shall attend each conference; decide questions of discipline, adopt measures to secure uniformity in their administration, and, when circumstances demand it, appoint fast and thanksgiving seasons, and counsel upon the general interests of the Church.

Organizing Mission-Conferences.

6. In conjunction with the Board of Missions, a bishop shall have power to organize mission-conferences.

Missionary Collection.

7. The bishops shall take a missionary collec-

tion and subscription during the session of each conference.

In Mission-Fields.

8. The bishops shall devote as much of their time as possible, consistent with other duties, to visiting our missions, exploring new fields, and working upon the general financial and educational interests of the Church.

Reports.

9. The bishops shall publish annually, in the columns of the *Religious Telescope* and *Frœhliche Botschafter*, reports of their respective districts, and also the amount of salary received from the several annual conferences in their charge.

Vacant Districts.

10. Should any district become destitute of a bishop by death or otherwise, the senior of the remaining bishops, on due notice of said fact, shall call together at some central point in the vacated district the delegates of the preceding General Conference from said bishop's district, who shall elect a bishop to fill the vacancy. The expenses of said delegates shall be provided for by the conferences to which they belong.

Annual Sermon.

11. It shall be the duty of the bishops to see that a suitable sermon be delivered to the preachers present at each annual conference.

Conference Superintendency.

12. The bishop last presiding at an annual con-

ference shall be regarded as the superintendent of
that conference for the ensuing year.

Delinquency.

13. When a bishop fails to perform his duty,
unless through unavoidable circumstances, he cannot be suffered to retain his office.

SECTION IX.

TRIAL OF PREACHERS.

Quarterly Conference Preachers.

The quarterly conference shall receive and try
all appeals, references, and complaints that may
come regularly before it ; but no member of quarterly conference can be suspended or expelled
from the Church prior to a committee trial. When
a quarterly conference preacher or exhorter is accused of any misdemeanor, the leader or steward
shall prosecute the case and shall inquire into the
nature of the complaints, and if there be grounds
for charges he shall present to the accused a copy
of the charges and notify him to choose a committee-man, and the prosecutor shall choose a
second committee-man; these two a third; and
this committee shall try the case, the preacher in
charge being chairman.

.If the accused refuse, or neglect, or fail, or is
unable to choose a committee-man after being
properly notified, the quarterly conference shall
choose a first and second person, and these two a
third, and this committee shall hear the case and

decide. If the accused is found guilty, he shall be silenced; provided, however, either party shall have the right of appeal to the next quarterly conference for a new trial.

Annual-Conference Preachers.

When a preacher, elder, or bishop is reported guilty of immorality, trespass, imprudent conduct, or disobedience to the order and Discipline of the Church, the preacher to whom it is known shall take with him another preacher, exhorter, or leader, and examine into the charge; but as the apostle saith (I. Tim. 5: 19), "Against an elder receive not an accusation, but before two or three witnesses." If it should appear that said reports are well founded, they shall be required to prefer charges against the accused; if not, they shall report to the next quarterly conference of which the accused is a member that they found no cause of action. If charges are preferred and no one be found willing to prosecute the case, then the said quarterly conference shall appoint a prosecutor, whose duty it shall be to notify the accused, in writing, of all the charges preferred against him. He shall also notify him to choose an elder as his committee-man, the prosecutor choosing an elder also as committee-man, in behalf of the Church, and they two a third elder or preacher, before which committee the case shall be tried. The prosecutor shall also notify the presiding elder of the district within whose bounds said cause of accusation occurred; and it shall be the duty of the presiding

5

elder to appoint the time and place of trial, giving
not less than twenty nor more than forty days' notice, to the parties concerned, of said trial; and he
shall also act as chairman in the case. Should a
majority of the committee be satisfied that the accusation is sustained, they shall require him to
hold his peace until the annual conference, where
he shall be accountable, and it shall be the duty of
the committee to transmit in writing the entire proceedings of said trial to the annual conference,
where the accused shall have a hearing before the
conference or a select committee thereof; and if
the findings are sustained, he shall be suspended,
expelled, or retained, as the conference may determine. But should the accused, after having been
duly notified, refuse or neglect to comply in choosing his committee-man and notifying the prose-
ecutor within fifteen days, the presiding elder
shall suspend him until the annual conference,
where, if he shall refuse to appear, he shall be
dealt with according to the judgment of the conference; provided, however, if he be an elder, elders only shall vote in the case; and, provided
further, that if the committee-men chosen by the
prosecutor and accused fail to agree as to the third
member of the committee, then the quarterly conference shall appoint said committee-man. If the
accused or prosecutor be a presiding elder or a
bishop, the presiding elder or bishop, as the case
may be, next adjoining, shall act as chairman on
the trial; provided, that in conferences having

only one presiding elder, the bishop shall appoint a chairman to act in the case.

The foregoing relates only to annual-conference members.

SECTION X.

TRANSFER OF PREACHERS.

A preacher desiring to remove his membership from one conference to another shall, when he applies for admission into the conference to which he goes, produce a transfer from the conference to which he formerly belonged, signed by the presiding officer, or published in the minutes of the conference from which he has been transferred.

Limit of Transfer.

A preacher or elder who receives a transfer is required to present said transfer to another conference, or return it to the conference by which it was issued, within two years after its date. Otherwise the transfer shall be null and void, and the name of the preacher shall be published as no longer connected with the Church as a minister.

Transferred Preachers—Where Accountable.

A preacher or elder receiving a transfer shall be a member of the quarterly conference in whose bounds he may reside, and also be accountable for his moral and official conduct to the annual conference granting said transfer until his transfer be received by the conference to which he has been transferred.

68 DISCIPLINE.

SECTION XI.

MARRIAGE—WHO MAY SOLEMNIZE.

All ordained ministers, and those that have obtained license from an annual conference, where the law of the State makes it the privilege of every regularly licensed minister to solemnize marriage, are authorized to solemnize marriage; but none having quarterly-conference license are permitted to solemnize marriage.

SECTION XII.

PREACHERS' DUTIES IN GENERAL.

The duties of preachers are to preach Christ crucified; to form classes, and report the same to the annual conferences; converse with the members on the spiritual condition of their souls; administer relief; strengthen and direct those that are afflicted and labor under temptations; animate the indolent; endeavor as much as possible to edify and instruct all in faith, in grace, and in the knowledge of Jesus Christ; visit the sick on all occasions; strive to enforce and confirm the doctrine they deliver by a well-ordered and exemplary life.

Directions to Preachers.

Let preachers heed the following directions:

1. Be diligent. Never trifle away your time. Always be serious. Let your motto be, "HOLINESS UNTO THE LORD." Avoid all vain conversation, converse sparingly, conduct yourself prudently with women, and demean yourself in all respects

as a true Christian. Be at all times averse to crediting evil reports. Believe evil of no one without good evidence. Put the best construction on everything.

2. Speak evil of no one. Whatever may be your thoughts, keep them within your own breast until you can tell the person concerned what you think wrong in his conduct.

3. Let your business be to save as many souls as possible. To this employment give yourself up wholly. Visit those who need it, and act in all things, not according to your own will, but as sons in the gospel ;'for as such it becomes your duty to employ your time in the manner prescribed, in preaching, and in visiting from house to house, in instruction and prayer, and in meditating on the word of God. With these be occupied until our Lord shall come.

Preachers Not to Trespass.

No preacher shall arbitrarily form a circuit, mission, or station within the limits of a circuit or presiding-elder district, or shall receive compensation for labor performed without the consent of the preacher in charge; nor shall any minister preaching in a different language accept a call from any regularly organized class or congregation which does not belong to his conference, without the consent of the annual conference to which the charge making the request may belong. Any preacher violating the provisions of this section shall be amenable to his quarterly or annual conference.

CHAPTER VII.
ITINERACY.
SECTION I.
ITINERANTS—HOW CONSTITUTED.

All who propose themselves without reserve, after having traveled two years under the direction of the stationing committee or presiding elder, and have been received, as such, by a vote of two-thirds of the members of conference, shall be recognized as itinerants.

Withdrawing from the Itineracy.

If anyone who is received, as above stated, shall cease to travel without giving satisfaction to the conference of which he is a member, he shall not be entitled to any support from the funds belonging to said conference. And, furthermore, he shall not re-enter the itineracy without the consent of at least two thirds of the conference. Yet supernumerary and superannuated relations shall be duly recognized as in accordance with this section, and may be secured to any brother having just claims thereto, by a vote of the conference.

Itinerant's Resignation.

Should a traveling preacher desire to leave the work assigned him, he must first acquaint the presiding elder of his intention, by writing; and should any one leave or neglect his station, except it be through sickness or other unavoidable circumstances, he shall be accountable to the next annual conference.

Stationing Itinerants.

The bishop and presiding elders of the past and present years shall constitute a stationing commit. tee, whose duty it shall be to supply all the circuits, stations, and missions, as far as practicable, from the list of itinerants; provided, however, that where there is but one presiding elder on the committee, the conference may elect to the same another elder from the elders not asking for work from said committee.

The stationing committee shall have at least two meetings before its work is completed.

Appeal from Stationing Committee's Report.

If any of the preachers thus stationed, or any who may not receive an appointment, are dissatisfied, they shall have a right to appeal to the annual conference. If two thirds grant the appeal * the decision shall be final.

Report of Stationing Committee.

The report of the stationing committee shall be read at least six hours before the adjournment of conference.

Limit of Pastorate.

No itinerant preacher shall be allowed to remain on the same station or circuit more than three consecutive years, unless with consent of the conference.

---

*NOTE.—In case of an appeal from the decision of the stationing committee, no preacher stationed by said committee shall be changed, without his consent, to accommodate the preacher asking such appeal.

Employment of Other Preachers.

Should there not be enough itinerants to fill all the circuits, stations, and missions, such vacancies shall be supplied by the stationing committee or presiding elders.

Fields of Labor.

A circuit or station shall not consist of any specific number of members or appointments; but when the annual conference judges it able to support a minister, it may be recognized as such.

SECTION II.
DUTIES OF ITINERANTS.

1.   It is the duty of an itinerant preacher to take the charge assigned him willingly, and to move to it if practicable.

2.   He shall attend the appointments on his circuit, preach to the people regularly, and hold class-meetings when practicable.

Correction of the Church Records.

3. He, in connection with the official members of each class, shall, at least one month before annual conference, correct the church records, and appoint a steward, subject to the approval of the class. No name shall be erased from the records until the disciplinary steps have been taken. He shall hold a meeting of the class and see that a class leader is elected.

Presiding at Trials.

4. He shall sit as president on the trial of members and see that a correct account of the same is kept.

Reports.

5. He shall render a strict account (as indicated in form) of his work at each quarterly conference, where he is to be held accountable for neglect of duty.

Circulation of Literature.

6. It shall be his duty to use every laudable effort to circulate our books and church periodicals, and to use due diligence to advance the interests of the Church printing establishment.

7. It shall be his duty to keep a list of the names of all the subscribers to our church periodicals, and the time of subscribing, at the different appointments on his circuit, and hand it over to his successor at the annual conference, with the list of the appointments. He shall also report the number of subscribers to our periodicals on his field of labor at each quarterly conference, and be examined by the presiding elder and quarterly conference as to whether he performs his duty in circulating the periodicals of the Church among the people of his charge.

Dismissal of Appointments.

8. No preacher shall dismiss any appointment from his circuit, or mission, without the consent of quarterly conference.

Records.

9. He shall procure a suitable book for a church-record, in which he shall register all the appointments and classes on his circuit, station, or mission, in their regular order, with the name of each

member attached to his or her class. He shall
also make a record of all the baptisms, marriages,
deaths, and proceedings of church trials, with the
names of all the parties in each case. He shall
report this record with the proceedings therein
to the last quarterly conference of each year for
approval or improvement. This book shall be the
property of the quarterly conference, and shall be
in addition to the regular class-books and circuit-
books.

General Collections.

10. It shall be the duty of preachers in charge
of circuits, stations, and missions to collect the
annual amount apportioned to their fields of labor
for the support of the bishops and presiding elders.

Missionary Collections.

11. He shall hold a general missionary meeting
at some convenient place on his work. He shall
also preach a missionary sermon, and appoint a
soliciting committee at every appointment, whose
duty it shall be, in conjunction with himself, to
canvass the church and community, personally, to
solicit funds for the missionary society. He shall
also keep a list of the names of contributors, as
far as possible, and report the same to conference
for publication, with the minutes, or in the annual
report of the Board of Missions, as the conference
may direct. He shall also establish monthly missionary prayer-meetings wherever practicable in
the societies of his charge. He shall be held to

striƈt account for the faithful performance of these duties.

Pastoral Visiting.

12. It shall be the duty of the preacher in charge of a station or circuit to give as much of his time as possible to visiting the families under his charge, and to pay striƈt attention to the young members under his care. We believe that this private work of visiting from house to house and exhorting the people is founded or implied in these solemn words of the apostle: "I kept back nothing that was profitable unto you, but have shewed you, and have taught you publicly, and from house to house." (Aƈts 20: 20.)

Evangelistic Work.

13. It shall be the duty of all preachers, whether local or itinerant, to make use of every laudable effort to enlarge the borders of our Zion, to spread scriptural holiness, and to report to théir respeƈtive annual conferences the number of new appointments obtained.

SECTION III.

PREACHERS' SALARIES.

1. The salary of a pastor shall be such amount as may be agreed upon between him and the quarterly conference of the field of labor to which he is sent. When a charge owns a parsonage, or rents a house for the pastor to live in, the charge shall have credit for thè same, by the pastor reporting as so much salary the amount the parsonage would rent for, or the amount paid for the rented house.

2.   A missionary employed by the Board of Missions shall receive such salary as in the judgment of the board may be proper.

3.   Preachers sustaining a superannuated relation, and their widows and orphans, shall be provided for by their respective·annual conferences, as their wants may require.

Parsonage and Moving of Preacher.

4.   It shall be the duty of a circuit or station, when a preacher is sent to it by annual conference, to provide a house and move said preacher at their own expense.

CHAPTER VIII.

APPEALS.

SECTION I.

FROM THE DECISION OF A CLASS.

Should any member be dissatisfied with the decision of a church or class, or committee of a church or class, an appeal may be had to the next quarterly conference by giving notice thereof to the preacher in charge, or the secretary of the trial, within thirty days after said trial, together with his reasons for such appeal; and it shall be the duty of the secretary to furnish the quarterly conference with a certified copy of the proceedings of the trial and of the notice of the appeal.

SECTION II.

FROM THE DECISION OF A QUARTERLY CONFERENCE.

Any exhorter or preacher dissatisfied with the decision of a quarterly conference may appeal to the ensuing annual conference within thirty days after the quarterly conference, by giving notice to the secretary, in writing, of his intention to appeal, together with his reason for so doing; and it shall be the duty of the secretary to furnish a certified copy of the proceedings, the notification and reasons assigned, to the annual conference.

SECTION III.
COURT OF APPEALS.

1. Any member of an annual conference, when dissatisfied with the decision thereof, shall have a right to appeal to a judicial court, which shall be constituted and governed as hereinafter stated.

2. Each annual conference, at the first session subsequent to the session of the General Conference, shall elect by ballot two members of the court, who shall hold office for four consecutive years.

3. In case of an appeal from an annual conference in form and manner hereinafter set forth, the presiding bishop of said conference shall at such time and place as he may determine, call together nine of the members of the court most accessible to the conference from which the appeal is taken, who thus called together shall constitute an appellate court to hear and determine said appeal.

4. This court shall organize by electing a chairman and some competent person as secretary.

5. The secretary shall receive and hold all papers and records pertaining to said appeal, subject to the order of the chairman; keep a true record

of all proceedings of said court, and certify the decision thereof to the annual conference from which the appeal is taken, and also to the appellant.

6. Seven of these members shall be necessary to constitute a quorum, and five must agree on a verdict, except in isolated conferences, where a quorum may consist of five only.

7. The decision of this court shall in all cases be final, except when· the objections are taken on the ground that the proceedings were irregular in the application of law, and said objections are entered before the verdict of the court is announced. In case of appeal from the court under this clause, the appellant must give notice within thirty days to the secretary of the court, who shall send a copy of all proceedings in said case to the General Conference.

8. In case of an appeal from the decision of an annual conference, the appellant must give written notice to the secretary of said conference, setting forth both his intent to appeal and the reasons for so doing.

9. On receipt of a notice of appeal, the secretary of the conference shall immediately notify the presiding bishop, and, on notice from said bishop, transmit a copy of the proceedings of the conference in said case to said court.

10. The necessary expenses incurred in the assembling of said court shall be provided for by each annual conference for its respective members of the court.

CHAPTER IX.

SECEDING MEMBERS.

Special Enactment.

Persons representing themselves as members of the Church of the United Brethren in Christ, and being insubordinate to the General Conference, and refusing to obey the order and discipline of the Church, as provided by the General Conference, shall be dealt with as follows:

1. In case of a presiding elder being suspended, or expelled, or who shall withdraw from the Church by joining another denomination, or connect himself with the minority body which seceded from the General Conference at York, Pa., May 13, 1889, and formed a new organization, it shall the duty of the presiding bishop of the district to appoint a successor to said presiding elder, and require him to take charge of the district forthwith.

2. If the offender be a pastor, it shall be the duty of the presiding elder of the district to appoint a successor, and require him to occupy said charge forthwith.

3. If the offender be a member of the quarterly conference, either minister or layman, he shall be declared by the presiding elder as having irregularly withdrawn from the Church, and his name shall be erased from the roll of the quarterly conference.

4. If the offender be a private member who has irregularly withdrawn from the Church by joining the said seceding organization, it shall be the duty

of the pastor to report the fact to the congregation and correct the roll of church-membership.

5. In the opening and organization of an annual conference or mission district, it shall be the duty of the presiding bishop to require the officer or member who calls the roll to record, as having irregularly withdrawn, the names of those who have connected themselves with said seceding party.

Provided, that if any persons thus affiliating shall, within a reasonable time, manifest a desire to return to their former relation as members of the Church, they may, with the consent of the local church, be reinstated.

CHAPTER X.
COURSES OF READING AND STUDY.
SECTION I.
QUARTERLY CONFERENCE PREACHERS.

It shall be the duty of each person receiving a quarterly conference license to preach to pursue the following course of study:

1. Outline Normal Lessons—Hurlbut.
2. Outline Bible Studies—Dunning.
3. The Bible; the Sunday-School Text Book—Holborn.
4. The Modern Sunday-School—Vincent.
5. A Primer of Christian Evidences—Redford.
6. The Seven Laws of Teaching—Gregory.
7. Progress of Doctrine in the New Testament—Bernard.

8. United Brethren Church History—Lawrence.
9. Theological Compend—Steele's Binney.
10. Outline Study of Man—Hopkins.

Examination.

At the fourth quarterly conference of each year, the presiding elder and pastor shall hold an examination in the above course.

All licentiates shall be required to complete the quarterly conference course of study before being admitted to the annual conference course of study.

Permanent License.

Any one completing the above course of study and passing a satisfactory examination in the same shall receive a license acknowledging that fact, which shall exempt him from annual renewal, so long as his doctine and deportment shall be conformable to the doctrine of Christ and the usages of our church.

SECTION II.

ANNUAL CONFERENCE PREACHERS.

Examinations.

All licentiate preachers are to be examined on the following course of study by the annual conference to which they belong. These examinations, as far as practicable, shall be in writing, and graded according to the following scale : 1. very good ; 2. good ; 3. medium ; 4. poor ; 5. very poor.

Licentiates shall be examined, also, each year of their probation, on the Bible and on the doctrine and government of the Church, as taught in our book of discipline, and shall also produce a

6

written sermon or essay. It is presumed that a fair knowledge of the ordinary branches of an English or German education has been acquired before entering upon this course. If the licentiate does not possess such knowledge, he shall be examined, each year, in grammar and geography.

First Year.

Dogmatics: Existence and Attributes of God; The Trinity; Creation and Providence. Pope, Vol. I.

Homiletics, parts I and II.—Etter.

Biblical History.—Blaikie.

Companion to the Bible.—Barrow.

Great Commission.—Harris.

Rhetoric.—Hart.

Second Year.

Dogmatics: Sin; Redemption; The Holy Ghost. Pope. Vol. II.

Homiletics, parts III and IV.—Etter.

Church History.—Fisher.

Mental Philosophy.—Haven.

Manual of Christian Evidences.—Fisher.

Elocution. —McIlvaine.

Third Year.

Dogmatics: Regeneration; Justification; Sanctification; The Church; The Christian Sabbath; The Sacraments; Last Things. Pope, Vol. III.

Pastoral Theology.—Shedd.

Logic.—Atwater.

The Beginnings of Christianity.—Fisher.

Analogy of Religion.—Butler.

Christian Ethics.—Gregory.

Doctrine of Christian Baptism.—Etter.

Books Recommended—Imitation of Christ, Kempis; Christian Doctrine, Weaver; Universal History, Barnes; Church History, Schaff; Foreign Missions, Pierson; Antiquities of the Jews, Josephus; History of Christian Doctrine, Sheldon; Theistic and Christian Belief, Fisher; History of the Reformation, Fisher; Fresh Light from the Monuments, Sayce; Parish Problems, Gladden; Modern Doubt and Christian Belief, Christlieb; Pastoral Theology. Hoppin; Biblical Geography, Hurlbut; Holy Living and Holy Dying, Taylor.

SECTION III.

GERMAN COURSE OF READING.

Quarterly-Conference Preachers.

FIRST YEAR.

Bible, Discipline, Kirchen-geshichte, Fletscher's Appelation, Nelson's Ursachen des Unglaubens. Hare's Rechtfertigung.

SECOND YEAR.

Bible; Discipline; D'Aubigne's Reformationgeschichte; Christlich-Apostolisches Glaubensbekenntniss, von Nast; Bekoempfung des Unglaubens, von Dr. Christlieb.

THIRD YEAR.

Bible; Discipline; Zeller's Seelenlehre; Philosophie des Erloesungs Plans; Nast Ueber die Gottheit Christi.

Annual Conference Preachers.

FIRST YEAR.

Kurtz's Abriss der Kirchen-Geschichte; Clark's Handbook; Sulzberger's Dogmatik — First Part; Fletcher's Appeal; Nelson on Infidelity; Hare on Justification; Nippert's Practical Theology; Wurst's Sprachlehre; written sermon—subject, Justification.

SECOND YEAR.

Bible; Wurst's Sprachlehre, continued; Sulzberger's Dogmatik—Part II; D'Aubigne's History of the Reformation; Zeller on the Soul; Philosophy of the Plan of Salvation; Luthardt's Apologetische Vorträge; written sermon—subject, The Christian Sabbath.

THIRD YEAR.

Bible; Discipline; Sulzberger's Dogmatik—Part III; Liscoe's Apostolic Creed; Oosterzee's Christologishe Betrachtungen, von Dr. Nast; Christliche Erfahrung, von Merrill; Pearson's Infidelity; Dr. A. Hülster's Psychology (Seelenlehre); written sermon—subject, Baptism.

SECTION IV.

Completing the Course.

Each licentiate is expected to complete the prescribed course within three years, unless a good reason exists for delay; provided, that any licentiate who has completed the full course of study in Union Biblical Seminary, and has passed the examination entitling him to a diploma of that institution, may be excused from examination in this course of study.

SECTION V.

Preparation for the Ministry.

We urge upon all who contemplate giving themselves to the gospel ministry the vital importance of completing a course of study in some one of our institutions of learning, and in addition, a course in Union Biblical Seminary. In exceptional cases wherein circumstances absolutely forbid such preparation, there should be the utmost diligence given to well-advised reading and study in order to successful work in the ministry. "Study to show thyself approved unto God, a workman that needeth not to be ashamed, rightly dividing the word of truth."

CHAPTER XI.
MEETING-HOUSES AND PARSONAGES.
Church-Houses.

Let all our meeting-houses be built plain and neat, with free seats, and not more expensive than necessary.

Trustees.

Boards of trustees of meeting-houses and parsonages shall in all cases have warranty deeds legally executed and made to them and their successors in office, in trust for the Church of the United Brethren in Christ, and shall have the same recorded in the county records where the property is situated.

Whenever it is contemplated by a local church to purchase or build a meeting-house, it shall be the duty of a leader or steward of said church to make it known to the quarterly conference of the circuit or station to which he belongs, whose duty

86 DISCIPLINE.

it shall be to appoint a judicious board of trustees, where the law of the state does not otherwise provide, of not less than three in number, or as the law of the state in which said house is to be built may direct; provided, however, that at least a majority of such board of trustees shall be members of our church. The trustees shall hold their office during the pleasure of the quarterly conference.

Building of Church-Houses and Parsonages.

No local church shall commence the building of any meeting-house or parsonage without first getting an act of incorporation, where the law of the state requires it. They shall form an estimate of the amount necessary to procure a lot, to build, and to make such other improvements as may be considered necessary. And they shall at no time proceed in incurring expenses beyond the means either in hand or sufficiently assured, so as to avoid involving our houses of worship and parsonages in any way by debt.

Duties of Trustees.

The trustees shall hold meetings annually, or oftener if need be, and shall elect from their number the following officers: namely, a president, secretary, and treasurer. The meetings of the board shall be subject to the call of the president. It shall be the duty of the secretary to keep a correct record of all the business transactions of the board in a book provided for that purpose, which shall at all times be open for inspection by the quarterly conference of the charge having the care of the property. The treasurer shall receive all funds for meeting-house, cemetery, and parsonage purposes, and pay out the same under the direction of the board, and report to the board the financial condition at their several meetings.

The board shall make an annual report to the quarterly conference.

Vacancies.

When a vacancy or vacancies occur in the Board of Trustees it shall be the duty of the quarterly conference to appoint a suitable person or persons to fill such vacancies, and to see that the records of the county wherein such board may reside shall correspond with the facts in the case, according as the law of the state may require, after such vacancy has been filled.

Abandoned Church-Houses.

When a house of worship ceases to be used by our own people for preaching or other religious purposes, it shall be the duty of the presiding elder of the district in which such house is located to report to the annual conference, which body shall have power to appoint a Board of Trustees who shall rent, lease, or sell such house of worship as they deem advisable, and report their proceedings to the annual conference, which body shall have power to use proceeds to pay debts on other houses of worship, build new houses, or turn the money into the funds of the Church-Erection Society, as

may seem proper at its own discretion; provided,
that in no case shall a church-house and its premises be sold without the consent of a majority of
the annual conference within whose bounds it is
located.

Abandoned Parsonages.

When the pastor refuses to occupy the parsonage, the question as to what disposition shall be
made of any revenues realized by renting the
property, or otherwise, shall be determined by the
quarterly conference.

Should any parsonage be permanently aban-
doned as such, the presiding elder of the district
in which such parsonage is located shall report the
same to the annual conference, which body shall
have power to appoint a board of trustees, who
shall rent or sell such parsonage, and pay over the
proceeds to the annual conference, which body
shall expend the same in paying debts on other
parsonages, or in building new ones within its
borders.

Transfer from German to English.

When a lot is deeded to an English United
Brethren church, or to a German United Brethren
church, and one or the other ceases to exist in an
organized form by deaths, removals, expulsions,
or otherwise, the church remaining shall have full
right to make such improvements or repairs on
said lot as may be needed for worship and a peaceable possession.

Division of Interests.

In cases where fields of labor having parsonages upon them are divided, the disposition of said parsonages shall be submitted to a board of arbiters, consisting of three members of the Church, one to be chosen by each quarterly conference, and the third by these two, to whom the whole matter shall be referred, their decision of the case being final. In cases where more than two quarterly conferences are interested, the same plan shall be pursued.

Real Estate.

Real estate held for church or parsonage purposes shall be subject to the same regulations as houses of worship and parsonages.

CHAPTER XII.
MORAL REFORM.
SECTION I.
TEMPERANCE.

Intoxicating Drinks.

1. The distilling, vending and using of intoxicating drinks as a beverage shall be and are hereby forbidden throughout our church, as are also the renting and leasing of property to be used for the manufacture or sale of such beverages, as also is the signing of petitions for license or the entering as bondsmen for persons engaged in the traffic of intoxicating drinks; and should any of our members or preachers be found guilty in these respects they shall be dealt with as in the case of other im-

moralities; provided, however, that this rule shall
not be so construed as to prevent druggists and
others from the vending or using of alcohol for
medicinal or mechanical purposes.

Tobacco.

We believe that the use of tobacco in any
form is injurious to physical health, and a need-
less waste of money which could and should be
otherwise employed; and we kindly advise our
members, especially our younger members, to
abstain from its use.

SECTION II.
SLAVERY.

All slavery, in every sense of the word, is totally
prohibited, and shall in no way be tolerated in our
church. Should any be found in our church who
hold slaves, they cannot continue as members
unless they do personally manumit or set free such
slaves.

And when it is known to any of our ministers in
charge of a circuit, station, or mission, that any of
its members hold a slave or slaves, he shall admonish such members to manumit such slave or slaves;
and if such persons do not take measures to carry
out the discipline, they shall be expelled by the
proper authorities of the Church; and any minister refusing to attend to the duties above described
shall be dealt with by the authorities to which he
is amenable.*

---

*This law, in its essential prohibitory features, was
adopted by the General Conference in 1821, Bishop Newcomer presiding.

SECTION III.

SECRET COMBINATIONS.

A secret combination is a secret league or con-federation of persons holding principles and laws at variance with the word of God and injurious to Christian character, as evidenced in individual life, and infringing upon the natural, social, political, or religious rights of those outside its pale.

Any member or minister of our church found in connection with such combination shall be dealt with as in other cases of disobedience to the order and discipline of the Church; in case of members, as found in Chapter IV., Section 3, and in case of ministers as found in Chapter VI., Section 9.

SECTION IV.

OATHS.

We believe that the mode of testifying to the truth when required so to do in a legal form, by way of affirmation, is on us solemnly, conscientiously and fully binding, before God, to tell the truth, the whole truth, and nothing but the truth.

SECTION V.

WAR.

We most positively record our disapproval of engaging in voluntary national aggressive warfare; yet we recognize the rightful authority of the civil government, and hold it responsible for the pres-ervation and defense of our national compact, against treason or invasion by any belligerent force, and we believe it to be entirely consistent with the spirit of Christianity to bear arms when called upon to do so by the properly constituted authorities of our government for its preservation and defense.

SECTION VI.

THE MARRIAGE RELATION.

1. We believe that the marriage relation is of divine authority; that it is the mutual union of one man and one woman; that the obligation is most sacred, and morally binding as long as both shall live, and therefore cannot be dissolved at will, nor should it be by a decree of a civil tribunal, except on evidence that one party is guilty of adultery.

2. On positive evidence of such guilt the innocent party is freed from further matrimonial obligations and justly entitled to a divorce.

3. We deny the right of marriage by virtue of a divorce obtained for other causes than adultery on the part of the person from whom the divorce is obtained, and therefore the right of the guilty party to remarry.

4. Any person sustaining a married relation contrary to that above recognized as justifiable shall be ineligible to the office of the ministry in this church.

5. Any minister of this church who shall knowingly solemnize the marriage of persons, either of whom has been divorced for other than the above justifiable cause, shall be amenable to the Church for disobedience to the order thereof.

CHAPTER XIII.

DOCTRINAL PUBLICATIONS.

Book Committee.

1. The editor of the *Religious Telescope*, the editor of the Sabbath-school literature, the editor of the German periodicals, the editor of the *Missionary Visitor*, and the publishing agent shall constitute a book committee, without whose sanction no book shall be published in the name of the Church or publishing house during the intervals of the General Conference.

Authorship of Doctrinal Publications.

2. No one of our preachers or laymen shall become the author of any doctrinal book or pamphlet, in a printed form, in the name of the Church, without the approbation of the book committee, or the annual conference, or of a committee chosen by the latter. And if any preacher or layman violates this rule, he shall be accountable to the class, or to the quarterly or annual conference, as the case may be.

CHAPTER XIV.

CHARTERS.

General Boards of Trustees.

1. The General Conference shall elect a board of trustees, consisting of twelve persons, who shall hold their office for four years, or until their successors are elected ; which board shall provide for the legal recognition of the General Conference, and secure the Church in all its property interests

by obtaining the proper articles of incorporation for said purpose.

Special Boards of Trustees.

2. The several boards of the Church, for their respective interests or institutions, shall secure suitable articles of incorporation.

Trustees of Church-Houses and Parsonages.

3. All boards of trustees of church-houses and parsonages, or real estate held as Church property, shall procure articles of incorporation according to the statutory provisions in force where the property is located, and according to the laws of the Church ; and at the second quarterly conference of each year, the presiding elders shall examine said boards as to the proper performance of this duty, and give such instruction as may be necessary.

Bequests.

4. Bequests for the benefit of the Church, not directed to any one of the special boards, shall be made to the TRUSTEES OF THE CHURCH OF THE UNITED BRETHREN IN CHRIST, to be managed or applied by them in harmony with the specified purpose of the donors, or, in the absence of such specification, to be administered according to the discretion of said board.

CHAPTER XV.

SABBATH-SCHOOLS.

SECTION I.

DUTY TO CHILDREN AND SABBATH-SCHOOLS.

1. For the benefit of the rising generation let those who are zealous for the welfare of their fel-

lows begin immediately, wherever children are found, to speak freely to them, and instruct them diligently, exhort them to love Jesus, and pray with them earnestly and plainly, that they may learn to know and remember their Creator in the days of their youth.

2. Wherever practicable, Sabbath-schools should be organized according to the constitution and by-laws herein contained.

Members' Duties.

3. It shall be the duty of all our members to encourage our Sabbath-schools by their presence when practicable, and always to lend them their aid and influence.

SECTION II.

GENERAL SABBATH-SCHOOL BOARD.

CONSTITUTION AND BY-LAWS.

ARTICLE I.

Name.

This shall be called the General Sabbath-school Board of the United Brethren in Christ.

ARTICLE II.

Composition.

This board shall be composed of five directors and one secretary, who shall be elected by the General Conference every four years. Two members of this board shall be laymen.

ARTICLE III.

Organization.

This board shall be organized by electing one of their number president, and some suitable person treasurer.

ARTICLE IV.

Object.

The object of this board shall be to promote the cause of Sabbath-schools in connection with our church and elsewhere, and thus, by our united efforts, to promote the glory of God and the happiness and salvation of mankind.

ARTICLE V.

Duties.

President.—The president shall have the general operations of the board under his care. He shall call meetings of the board when necessary, and present the wants of the board ; and he shall sign all orders drawn on the treasurer for the use of the board, as appropriated by it.

Secretary.—The secretary shall keep a record of all the business transactions of the board, conduct its correspondence, report to it annually or oftener if desired, and make such reports for it to the General Conference as may be required and if practicable, at the request of the board, devote his whole time to its interests.

Treasurer.—The treasurer shall take charge of and hold in trust all the funds and papers of value belonging to the board, subject to its direction and the written order of the president.

ARTICLE VI.

Meetings, Powers, Duties.

Meetings of the board shall be held annually, or oftener if need be, at the call of the president, to provide ways and means for the successful operation of its plans. It shall appropriate money to defray all necessary expenses, and no money shall be paid out of its funds except by its express order. It shall have power to fill vacancies in its numbers, and to employ any suitable person or persons to perform needed services for the advancement of its objects under its direction. It shall also, through its secretary, make quadrennial reports to the General Conference.

ARTICLE VII.

Appropriations.

The funds of the board shall be used as follows:

1. To assist in organizing and sustaining Sabbath-schools in such localities and in such manner as may be advisable.

2. To conduct the business and ca⁻rv forward the work of the board.

Applications for Aid.

3. When aid is needed, those making the application shall first organize a United Brethren Sabbath-school by adopting the disciplinary regulations of the Church, and shall report the fact to the secretary, as well as the kind and amount of help needed; and upon a favorable consideration of the application, such supplies as may be considered necessary and advisable shall be furnished. Such donations shall, however, be discontinued unless a church-organization shall be effected after a reasonable time.

7

SECTION III.

ANNUAL-CONFERENCE RELATIONS AND DUTIES.

Officers.

1. Each conference shall annually elect one person who shall be Sabbath-school secretary and treasurer, who shall be an advisory member of the General Sabbath-school board, and whose duty it shall be to give diligent attention to all the interests of this board before the conference; to receive and transmit the funds for this board to the treasurer thereof; to be faithful in correspondence with the secretary of this board; to hold at a convenient time during the session a Sabbath-school anniversary for the purpose of advancing the Sabbath-school cause.

Pastors' Duties.

2. The pastor shall have general supervision of all the Sabbath-schools on his charge. It shall be his duty to be present at all sessions of the Sabbath-school as far as practicable ; to preside at all business meetings when present, and at all meetings for the organization of Sabbath-schools. He shall organize a Sabbath-school at each appointment on his charge, where there is not one already; he shall preach on the subject at each appointment at least once a year; he shall report to his conference the number of schools, the number of officers and teachers employed, the number of scholars enrolled, the number of conversions among the scholars, the number of schools continuing through the year, and the amount of money collected for

the use of schools, for the general fund, for missions, and for any other purpose.

SECTION IV.

ORGANIZATION OF SABBATH-SCHOOLS.

In order to insure unity in administration and
soundness of teaching, all our Sabbath-schools
shall, as far as possible, conform to the following:

Organizing Sabbath-Schools.

1. Any preacher or member of this church may
organize a United Brethren Sabbath-school outside
of a regular pastoral charge by calling a meeting of
the members of the Church, together with other
friends of Sabbath-schools, in any community
where practicable, and organize by enrolling all
who will agree to unite in such organization, and
proceed to elect, by ballot or otherwise, a superintendent and other necessary officers; provided,
however, that none be allowed to vote who are
under twelve years of age.

Officers.

2. The superintendent and other general officers
of the school shall hold their respective offices one
year, or until their successors shall have been appointed in the manner prescribed in the constitution.

Superintendent's Duties.

3. The superintendent shall render to each quarterly conference an account of the condition of his
school, stating also whether he is prompt in opening and orderly in his management of the same,
and at the close of his term he shall see that a suc-

cessor is selected after the manner prescribed; pro vided, that on stations where it shall be thought best by the pastor, the quarterly conference may elect the superintendent.

Dismissal of Superintendent.

4. The quarterly conference shall have power to dismiss a superintendent for immoral conduct, heresy, or insubordination.   _

SECTION V.

SABBATH-SCHOOLS AND THE MISSIONARY WORK.

Each of our Sabbath schools is hereby constituted an auxiliary to the branch missionary society, within whose limits it is located; and the superintendent is expected to take a collection at least once each quarter for the cause of missions, and report the amount to the pastor or branch treasurer. Any member may become a life member of the auxiliary by the payment of three dollars, and shall be entitled to a certificate of life membership.

SECTION VI.

FORM OF CONSTITUTION FOR A SABBATH-SCHOOL.

The following is recommended as a suitable form for the constitution of a United Brethren Sabbath-school:

ARTICLE I.

.This school shall be known as the United Brethren Sabbath-school of ———.

ARTICLE II.

The object of the school shall be to gather in all, both old and young, as far as possible, for instruction in and the study of the Bible, and to promote the worship of God, and to secure the salvation of precious souls.

ARTICLE III.

1. The officers shall be the pastor, a superintendent, a secretary, a treasurer, a librarian, and, when desired by the school, a chorister and organist. The duties of these officers shall be such as usually pertain to such offices ; and whenever it is generally deemed necessary for the interests of the school, an assistant may be elected to each of these offices, each of whom shall be subject in his official duties to his superior officer, except in the absence of such superior.

2. There shall also be an executive committee of three—or five, as the school may prefer—including the superintendent and pastor, who shall be members *ex officio ;* and a majority of this committee shall be members of the United Brethren Church at ———.

3. The superintendent, when at all possible, shall be a member of the United Brethren Church, in good and regular standing.

4. When a superintendent is to be chosen, the official members of the church shall present to the school the names of at least two suitable persons for superintendent, and the one receiving the highest number of votes shall be declared elected; provided, that the election shall be by ballot, and only enrolled members of the school, above twelve years of age, shall be allowed to vote. The secretary,

treasurer, librarian, chorister, and organist shall be elected by the school. The teachers shall be appointed by the superintendent, with the approval of the pastor.

5. The pastor of the church shall preside at each annual election, whenever practicable, and the superintendent or pastor shall preside at all special elections.

ARTICLE IV.

Vacancies for unexpired terms shall be filled in the manner and form as above provided for annual re-organization. The Executive Committee, provided for in Division two, Article three, shall be, except the pastor and superintendent, who shall be *ex-officio* members thereof, chosen annually by the officers and teachers of the school.

ARTICLE V.

It shall be the duty of the Executive Committee, with the pastor and superintendent, to select and order suitable literature and helps for the school from time to time, and to devise and put in operation plans for raising necessary funds for this purpose.

SECTION VII.

1. All Sabbath-schools shall be governed by the foregoing constitution, provided, that any school may have the privilege of enacting such by-laws for its better regulation as will not conflict with said constitution.

2. The place of meeting for the Sabbath-school shall be in the usual place of meeting for the

United Brethren church services, and at such hours of the day as shall not interfere with the other church·services.

CHAPTER XVI.

CONSTITUTION OF THE MISSIONARY SOCIETY.

Name.

I. This society shall be called the "Home, Frontier, and Foreign Missionary Society of the United Brethren in Christ," and is organized for the purpose of aiding the annual conferences in extending their missionary labors throughout the country, and into foreign and heathen lands.

Life Members and Directors.

II. The payment of ten dollars at one time shall constitute a life member, or fifty dollars at one time a life director. No certificate of life membership or life directorship shall be granted until the full amount is paid.

Officers.

III. The officers of this society shall consist of the bishops of the Church, who shall be officers *ex officio*, the senior bishop being president, and the other bishops ranking as vice-presidents according to seniority; also a secretary and treasurer, who shall be elected every four years by the General Conference. The General Conference shall also elect every four years seven directors, who, in connection with the above-named officers, shall constitute the Board of Directors.

Duties of Officers.

IV. The president shall preside at all meetings of the board, and shall have power, in conjunction with the secretary, to call special meetings. In the absence of the president, one of the vice-presidents shall fill his place.

V. The secretary shall keep a correct record of all the proceedings of the Society, conduct its correspondence, and devote himself exclusively to the interests of the Society. He shall keep a record of all the life members, life directors, legacies, etc. He shall also make out and publish, under the direction of the board, an annual report of the whole missionary work ; also a quadrennial report to the General Conference. His salary shall be determined by the board, and reported to the ensuing General Conference.   /

VI. The treasurer shall hold the funds of the society, subject to the order of the board, and, at the discretion of the board, devote himself exclusively to the interests of the Missionary Society.

Board of Directors.

VII. The Board of Directors shall hold annual meetings ; have power to appoint an executive committee, consisting of five members ; make by-laws to regulate its own business ; appropriate money to defray incidental expenses ; employ missionaries and agents ; open new missions ; make appropriations to mission-conferences ; employ laborers for mission-districts ; dissolve mission-conferences ; fill vacancies in its own body ; in connection with the bishops or any one of them, ordain ministers to the office of elder; and publish, at our own press, such matter as the cause may from time to time demand.

Mission Districts.

VIII. A mission-district shall consist of two or more fields of labor, outside the bounds of an annual conference. Its annual sessions shall be presided over by a bishop, or an elder appointed by the Board of Missions. At these annual meetings the boundaries of fields of labor shall be fixed, the character of members examined, preachers may be received, examined and passed on course of reading, and be ordained. A presiding elder may be elected, if the Board of Missions so advise, and ministers appointed to fill the fields of labor by the presiding officer and the presiding elder.

Missionaries.

IX. Each missionary in the employ of the board shall report quarterly to the secretary the condition of his mission; and no missionary shall be entitled to his salary who shall neglect to comply with this requirement, or leave his work without the consent of the Executive Committee or the Board of Missions, or his presiding elder. The presiding elders of mission-conferences shall report quarterly the condition of their respective works.

Branch Officers.

X. Each conference shall be considered a branch of this society, and shall elect a treasurer and secretary.

Treasurer.

1. The branch treasurer shall hold the funds designed for the board, subject to its order.

Secretary.

2. The branch secretary shall keep a record of the proceedings of the annual conference in relation to home, frontier, and foreign missions, separately, and report the same *immediately* after the session of the conference to the secretary of the board. He shall report the number of missions, appointments, meeting-houses, members at the beginning of the year, members received, and members remaining; Sabbath-schools, scholars, and teachers; what paid on missions as salary, what collected for missions on missions; what collected for missions in the whole conference; how much paid the parent board, and how much paid to home missions; and the names and *post-office* addresses of life directors and life members. The branch secretaries shall be responsible to their respective annual conferences for the faithful discharge of their duties.

Object of Contributions.

XI. The branch societies, or individual members, may specify to what particular portion of the work their funds shall be applied ; provided, however, that if more is thus designated than is necessary for the work specified, it may be applied to some other work, as the board shall determine.

Home Missions.

XII. Each branch society shall have the exclusive management of the home missions within its own limits; provided, however, that the missionary board shall be permitted to open and operate missions within the bounds of any annual conference, jointly or independently, by the consent of such conference.

Treasurer's Security to Boards.

XIII. Treasurers of the parent board and of the branch society shall give approved security.

Bequests.

XIV. All bequests and donations, the interest of which is to go to missionary purposes, made to any of the above societies, shall be kept sacred.

Mission-Conferences.

XV. No mission-conference shall be formed with less than ten ministers and eight hundred lay members; and any territory hereafter occupied with less than the above number of members shall be constituted a mission-district.

Formation of Self-supporting Conferences.

XVI. The bishops shall recommend annually to the Board of Missions which, if any, mission-conferences shall become self-supporting, and on the approval of the Board of Missions shall give notice to said conference one year before being made self-supporting.

Territory of Mission-Conferences.

XVII. The Board of Missions is permitted to occupy any territory within the bounds of an annual conference not occupied by said conference.

Local Societies.

XVIII. Section i. Local societies may be organized in any United Brethren congregation v
securing names and electing officers.

Sec. 2. The officers of these societies shall be
a president, vice-president, secretary, and treasurer.

Sec. 3. The object of these societies shall be 'o
enlist and educate the membership, especially 'he
young people, in missionary work in the home
and foreign field.

Sec. 4. The treasurer shall hold all the funds of
the society and transmit the same through ;he
pastor of the charge annually to the branch society.

Sec. 5. Any person may become a member of a
local society upon such terms as said society shall
designate.

Sec. 6. All societies shall hold quarterly meetings for the purpose of transacting business, securing money, and cultivating a spirit of Christian
missions.

CHAPTER XVII.
WOMAN'S MISSIONARY ASSOCIATION.
Articles of Incorporation.

1. The name by which this corporation shall be
known is, "The Woman's Missionary Association
of the United Brethren in Christ," and the said
organization is not for profit.

2. The principal business of the said corporation

is to be transacted in the city of Dayton, county of Montgomery, State of Ohio.

3. Said corporation is formed for the purpose of engaging and uniting the efforts of women in sending missionaries into the foreign and domestic fields of the United Brethren Church, and supporting said missionaries and other laborers in said mission-fields, and in securing by gift, bequest, and otherwise, the funds necessary for the purpose aforesaid.

4. Said corporation is not to have capital stock.

BY-LAWS.

BY-LAW I.

Membership.

The payment of one dollar annually shall constitute membership in the association, and the payment of ten dollars at one time, life membership. The payment of twenty-five dollars at one time shall constitute the donor a life director. By the installment plan the payment of two dollars annually for five years constitutes life membership, or five dollars annually for five years a life directorship. A certificate is given at the time of payment in full.

BY-LAW II.

Organization.

The organization of this society shall consist of a board of managers, nine trustees, and branch and local associations, to be organized under the constitution hereto attached.

BY-LAW III.
Board of Managers.

The Board of Managers shall consist of three delegates from each branch association, who shall be elected at the branch annual meeting, held within three months of the annual meeting of the board. Said board shall meet in the First United Brethren Church of Dayton, Ohio, at the time of the meeting of the Home, Frontier, and Foreign Missionary Society, in May, 1876, and annually thereafter, at such time and place as they may from time to time designate.

The duties of said board shall be advisory to trustees. Life directors of the association shall be regarded as advisory members of the Board of Managers.

BY-LAW IV.
Duties of the Board of Trustees.*

The Board of Trustees shall have power to select locations for missions, appoint missionaries, appropriate the funds of the association as the interest of the cause may demand, and attend to the administration and general management of the affairs of the association.

BY-LAW V.
Relation of the Society to the Church.

This society shall work in harmony with the

---

*Trustees to be elected by members of the association, who shall vote either in person or by proxy, the first Thursday in June, in the city of Dayton. The officers shall be elected by the trustees.

Home, Frontier, and Foreign Missionary Society of the United Brethren in Christ, and under the direction of the General Conference of said Church; and its missionaries shall be subject to the same rules that govern the missionaries of the aforesaid missionary society.

BY-LAW VI.
Funds.

All funds coming into the hands of the treasurer of the association will be held subject to the order of the Board of Trustees; and no funds shall be disbursed by the treasurer except upon the orders of said Board, duly signed by the secretary

BY-LAW VII.
Branch Societies.

One branch society may be formed within the bounds of any annual conference of the United Brethren Church, by the adoption of the branch constitution.

BY-LAW VIII.
Amendments.

These by-laws may be altered or amended at any annual meeting of the Board of Managers by a vote of two-thirds of the members present.

BRANCH CONSTITUTION.
ARTICLE I.

This society shall be called the ——— Conference Branch of the Woman's Missionary Association of the United Brethren in Christ.

ARTICLE II.

The object of this society is to aid the association to awaken an interest among women in behalf of Christian missions, and to raise funds for their support.

ARTICLE III.

The membership of this society shall consist of the members of the association within the limits of this conference district.

ARTICLE IV.

Section 1.   The officers of this society shall be a president, two vice-presidents, a secretary, and a treasurer, who, together, shall constitute an executive committee to supervise the entire work of the association within the conference district.   It shall be their duty to make earnest efforts to secure the organization of local societies in all the United Brethren congregations within the bounds of the conference.

Sec. 2.   It shall be the duty of the secretary of this society to keep a correct record of its proceed ings and the proceedings of the Executive Com· mittee, and transmit a report of the same, with the number of members, to the recording secretary o the Board of Managers at least ten days before the annual meeting of the board.

Sec. 3.   It shall be the duty of the treasurer to receive and hold the funds of the society, and trans· mit the same semi-annually to the treasurer of the board, the last report to be sent in at least ten days before the meeting of the Board of Managers.

ARTICLE V.

This society shall hold annual meetings to elect

its officers and members of the Board of Managers, and to transact any business pertaining to its work, its members to consist of the officers and three delegates from each local society.

ARTICLE VI.

This society shall provide for the expenses of its delegates to the annual meeting of the Board of Managers.

ARTICLE VII.

Life members within the bounds of ——— Conference shall be regarded as advisory members of the annual meeting of this society.

LOCAL CONSTITUTION.

ARTICLE I.

This society shall be called the ——— Local Society of ——— Branch Society of the Woman's Missionary Association of the United Brethren in Christ; and any woman may become a member of the same by consenting to the by-laws of said association.

ARTICLE II.

The officers of this society shall consist of a president, vice-president, secretary, and treasurer, and two or more collectors.

ARTICLE III.

Section 1. The duties of the president shall be those usual to the office.

Sec. 2. It shall be the duty of the vice-president to assume the duties of the president in her absence.

8

Sec. 3. It shall be the duty of the secretary to keep a record of the proceedings of each meeting, with the names of members, and report quarterly to the secretary of the branch society.

Sec. 4. It shall be the duty of the treasurer to hold all funds of the society and transmit the same semi-annually to the treasurer of the branch so· ciety.

Sec. 5. It shall be the duty of the collectors to visit members of the Church and solicit names collect quarterly dues, and report the number of visits and amount collected at each meeting.

ARTICLE IV.

Any child may become a member of this society upon the payment of — cents per quarter.

ARTICLE V.

This society shall meet quarterly, and shal. arrange its year with reference to the annual meeting of the branch society.

CHAPTER XVIII.
CHURCH-ERECTION SOCIETY.
Name.

I. This society shall be known as "The Church-Erection Society of the Church of the United Brethren in Christ," and is organized for the purpose of aiding feeble churches in the erection of houses of worship.

Officers.

ARTICLE II.

The officers of this society shall consist of a president, three or more vice-presidents, a corresponding secretary, a treasurer, and five directors.

The senior bishop of the Church shall be president, *ex officio*, the three or more other bishops of the Church shall be vice-presidents, *ex-officio*, and be eligible to the presidency in the order of their election to the office of bishop. .

The corresponding secretary shall be elected by the General Conference.

The treasurer of the Missionary Society shall be the treasurer of the Church-Erection Society. The five directors shall be elected by the General Conference. These officers and directors shall constitute a Board of Directors, and shall be elected every four years by the General Conference.

ARTICLE III.

Duties of Officers.

Section 1. The president shall preside at all meetings of the board, and shall have power, in conjunction with the secretary and two directors, to call special meetings. In the absence of the president, one of the vice-presidents shall fill his place.

Sec. 2. The corresponding secretary shall keep a record of the proceedings of the society, conduct its correspondence, and devote himself to the work of securing funds, and otherwise attending to the interests of the society. He shall also make up and publish, under the direction of the board, an annual report of the whole church-erection work; also a quadrennial report to the General Conference.

Sec. 3. The treasurer shall hold the funds of the society subject to the order of the board, and make and publish annual reports to the board, and quadrennial reports to the General Conference.

Sec. 4. The Board of Directors shall hold annual meetings, appoint an executive committee consisting of the corresponding secretary, treasurer, and three directors, or of the president and two directors, or of one of the vice-presidents and two directors, or of the president and one vice-president and one director; make by-laws to regulate its business; lend money to churches; appropriate money to defray incidental expenses; fill vacancies in its own body, and publish such matter from time to time as the cause may require.

Sec. 5. Each conference in the Church is hereby constituted a branch of this society, and required to elect annually a branch secretary and a branch treasurer, who shall respectively discharge the duties usually devolving on such officers.

. *Apportionment and Division.*

ARTICLE IV.

It shall be the duty of each annual conference to make a judicious assessment to the several fields of labor for this interest, which fund, when collected, shall be divided equally, the branch treasurer retaining one half for the conference and transmitting the other half to the treasurer of the parent society; provided, however, that special donations and bequests shall all go to the parent society unless the donor directs otherwise.

Receipts of Treasurer.

ARTICLE V.

The treasurer of the parent Board of Missions shall receipt for all moneys sent him by the various conference treasurers, that they may make settlement with their respective annual conferences.

Application for Aid.

ARTICLE VI.

Application for aid from this society must be made to the Board of Managers, through the bishop, and the presiding elder of the district and the preacher in charge of the circuit, station, or mission where such house is to be erected, who shall state in writing the condition of the local church desiring such aid, the prospects of success, and the security of the investment.

Return of Loans.

ARTICLE VII.

Should any local church thus aided lose its organization, so as to make the sale of such house necessary, then, out of the proceeds of such sale, the amount loaned, with interest, shall be refunded to the Church-Erection Board.

Granting of Loans.

ARTICLE VIII.

Section 1. The board shall make no appropriations where there is reasonable prospect that the church asking aid can succeed without it; or where there is no prospect of building up a good membership.

Sec. 2. All aid rendered shall be only as a loan, the principal to be refunded without interest, at such times as the board may direct, but in no case for a longer term than five years at any one time, or more than five hundred dollars to any individual or single church—except that in large, growing towns and cities, at the discretion of the board, the amount may be increased to $1,000 and the time extended to ten years.

Sec. 3. Moneys shall not be loaned to any church until their church-property is secured by deed as provided for in Discipline; nor shall moneys be loaned to churches until their trustees have forwarded an abstract of the title of their property and their notes, secured by first mortgage on the premises and properly recorded in the records of the courts for the inspection of the Board of Managers or Executive Committee.

Insurance.
ARTICLE IX.

The trustees of churches which receive moneys from the Church-Erection Society shall be required to secure said church-buildings from loss by fire in some reliable insurance company.

ARTICLE X.
Special Agents.

The Board of Managers may employ one or more special agents; provided, however, that said agency shall not be continued for a longer term than three months, unless it be apparent that said agency is a moneyed success to the society.

CHAPTER XIX.
PRINTING ESTABLISHMENT.
Name.

1. The above establishment shall be called "The Printing Establishment of the United Brethren in Christ."

Election of Officers.

2. The legislative authority herein granted shall be vested in the General Conference of said church, whose duty it shall be to elect the necessary officers not otherwise provided for, and make or amend any rules as in their judgment may seem expedient.

Proceeds.

3. The proceeds of said establishment, over and above contingent expenses, shall be applied to the benefit of traveling and worn-out preachers, and their widows and orphans. The distribution of any available profits of the publishing house for this purpose shall be in proportion to the number of regular ministers in each annual conference who are *itinerants*, according to the "Itinerant Plan" of the Discipline. It shall be the duty of the secretaries of the annual conferences each year to report to the publishing agent at Dayton, Ohio, the true number of such itinerants as found upon the records of the several conferences; also the name and address of the conference treasurer appointed to receive the dividend awarded to his conference.

Trustees.

4. A board of nine trustees, elected by the Gen-

eral Conference, shall take the oversight of the establishment. They shall meet annually, and oftener if need be, on the call of the president, in the publishing house at Dayton, Ohio.

Officers.

5. The officers of the establishment shall consist of nine trustees, one agent, and such number of editors as the General Conference shall deem necessary.

Duties of Trustees.

6. It shall be the duty of the trustees to fix the salaries of agent and editors, to make settlement with the officers of the establishment every six months, and see that they properly discharge their duties, and, if found derelict, may suspend them from office until the General Conference ; provided, no such officers shall be suspended until they have been furnished with a copy of the complaints in writing, and have had an opportunity of defense before the Board of Trustees. They shall also have the privilege of making any by-laws which may seem expedient for the better regulation of the minor concerns of the office; provided, they do not violate any part of the foregoing rules. They shall elect an executive committee, a majority of which shall consist of members of the board. This committee shall take oversight of the house during the intervals of the meetings of the board, and examine the books and accounts of the establishment every six months.

Duties of Agent.

7. It shall be the duty of the agent to take charge of the temporal concerns of the office, furnish such material as may be needed, and to act as the general book agent under the direction of the Board of Trustees. He shall prepare and publish a report annually, through the *Religious Telescope* and *Joyful Messenger*, and shall also make a report to the General Conference. It shall be his duty to make arrangements for *verbatim* reports of the proceedings of the General Conference for publication.

Vacancies.

8. Should a vacancy occur in any of the offices of the establishment, or in the Board of Trustees, the trustees may fill said vacancy, until the sitting of the next General Conference.

Employment of Time.

9. No editor or officer employed in the establishment shall accept any office or engage in any business which will interfere with the duties of his office.

CHAPTER XX.
EDUCATIONAL INSTITUTIONS.
I. BOARD OF EDUCATION.

Section 1. There shall be a general board of education, known by the name of "The Board of Education," under the care of the General Conference of the Church of the United Brethren in Christ. This board shall consist of twelve members, elected by the General Conference, who shall hold office for four years, six of whom shall be clergymen; the remainder may be lay members of the United Brethren Church. Five members, including the president or vice-president, shall constitute a quorum.

Officers.

Sec. 2. The officers shall be a president, vice-president, recording secretary, corresponding secretary, and treasurer. These shall be elected by the members of the board at their first regular meeting after the sitting of the General Conference, and shall hold office until the next regular session of the General Conference.

The board may elect any competent persons, members of the United Brethren Church, to be their treasurer and corresponding secretary; these, if elected outside of the board, shall be advisory members of the board.

The corresponding secretary is to devote such portion of his time to the work of the board as it may direct, his compensation to be fixed by the board.

In case of vacancy occurring in the board, by death or otherwise, the board shall have power to fill the vacancy, the election to be by ballot, and the person elected to hold office until the next meeting of the General Conference.

There shall be at least one session of the board each year. Meetings of the board shall be called by the president, upon request of three members.

Objects.

Sec. 3. The objects of this board shall be:

Beneficiary Aid.

(1.) To raise funds by collection, donation, bequest, or otherwise, to aid by loan, without interest, as the Executive Committee may determine, in educating, in both their collegiate and theological courses, pious young persons who are preparing themselves for the work of the gospel ministry, or as missionaries in the United Brethren Church; provided, however, the board shall have power to receive money and use it for other educational purposes, as donors may direct.

Publications.

(2.) To seek by the publication of tracts, pamphlets, addresses, or books upon educational questions, to diffuse among our members a more general knowledge of the value of a sanctified education and of a well-instructed ministry, and thereby awaken in them a better appreciation of our institutions of learning, and of the obligations resting upon them to give of their substance for their support.

Reports and Recommendations.

(3.) To make an annual report of the condition, financially and otherwise, of the colleges and other educational institutions of the Church; to make such recommendations to the managers of these institutions as will tend to make them more efficient; to secure, as far as may seem desirable, harmony of courses of study between preparatory schools, and colleges and universities.

(4.) To discourage the multiplication of schools and colleges when they cannot be properly supported. Conferences, or a conference, wishing to establish, relocate or change the grade of a school, shall first counsel with the Board of Education, both as to the advisability of the act proposed, and also as to method and location, and any school started without the sanction of this board shall not be recognized as a Church-school.

Collections.

4. To accomplish these results, the board may cause an annual collection to be taken on the next Sabbath following the last Thursday of January, or at such other time as the presiding elder of the dis trict* may deem most suitable. The preacher in charge, or some other competent person, shall first preach a sermon or make appropriate remarks concerning the object, plans, and working of this board, and then take a collection in such manner as will secure the largest amount of funds. If the board thinks best, it may apportion the amount to be raised by the various conferences, according to their number and ability, and these in turn shall apportion to their respective fields of labor, and the funds thus raised shall be sent to the treasurer of the board.

Recommendation for Aid.

·5. Young persons aided by this board must first be recommended as suitable persons to receive aid, by the conference in whose bounds they live, or to which they belong, or by the Board of Missions when the applicant does not reside within the bounds of any conference, or by an educational committee appointed by saíd conference, to whom all requests for aid, not acted upon by conference, or which shall occur during the interim of its sittings, shall be referred.

Honorary Members.

6. The board shall have power to make persons honorary members of the same on the payment of fifty dollars. The persons thus made honorary members shall have the right to sit in the meetings of the board and engage in its deliberations, but shall have no right to vote.

Executive Committee.

7. The board shall have power to appoint an executive committee from its own body, and to make such by-laws to regulate its own proceedings, and to effectually accomplish the object of its creation, as shall not be inconsistent with this constitution.

Quadrennial Report.

8. The board, through its corresponding secretary, shall make to the General Conference a report of all the work done during the preceding four years, including money received by collections, bequests, or otherwise, the amount paid out, and the purposes for which it was paid. The board may propose to the General Conference, from time to time, such plans as it may consider useful or necessary for the success of the work committed to it.

Amendment.

9. No addition or amendment to the provisions of this constitution shall be made unless by consent of a majority of the members of the General Conference present at any of the sessions. Notice of this proposed addition or amendment shall have been given at least one day previous.

II. ACADEMIES.

In this day of excellent high school systems in many parts of our country, academies should be located very judiciously, and should confine their courses of study to such branches of learning as will prepare for entrance upon the freshmen or sophomore year of the best colleges. A first-class academy is exceedingly better than a second or third-class college. Any institution that does not succeed as an academy is not likely with similar facilities to prosper as a college. No new academy should be undertaken with a less sum than twenty-five thousand dollars.

III. COLLEGES.

1. The success of our church work is connected very vitally with the colleges of the Church. In these our youth are developed and equipped in mind and heart for the work of efficient service to humanity.

The ministry and laity should earnestly use their power to have as many young people as possible attend our own institutions of learning and to encourage persons to give liberally of their means for the more thorough establishment and equipment of our educational institutions.

2. For the purpose of greater unity and efficiency in our educational work, the General Conference recommends that the length of a course of study leading to degrees be three years in the preparatory department and four years in the college, and asks all the schools in the Church to adopt this standard as soon as possible.

3. No college should be founded without an imperative necessity, and with a less sum of money than one hundred thousand dollars, of which fifty thousand dollars shall be a permanent and productive endowment. As to Christian education, the divine word aptly declares: "Wisdom is a defense, and money is a defense: but the excellency of knowledge is, that wisdom giveth life to them that have it."

IV. UNION BIBLICAL SEMINARY.

1. This institution of sacred learning, located at Dayton, Ohio, is maintained by the United Brethren in Christ for the purpose of educating persons called of God to the work of the ministry, and the spread of the gospel of Christ among men. It shall be under the control of the General Conference of the United Brethren in Christ, by which the officers shall be elected at each quadrennial session.

Directors.

2. The Board of Directors shall be composed of fifteen trustees, ten of whom shall be elected by

the General Conference, and five of whom shall be elected by the Board of Directors for a term of two years each, and the bishops of the Church, who shall be considered as *ex-officio* members; provided always, that a majority of the trustees thus elected must be *bona fide* residents of the State of Ohio.

Duties of Directors.

3. The Board of Directors shall meet on the call of the senior bishop immediately after their election, and organize by electing a president and secretary. They shall meet annually in the semi-nary building at Dayton, Ohio, elect the necessary faculty, review the work of the General Manager and the faculty, determine their salaries, and give general directions to the management of the institution.

The Board of Directors may fill any vacancy caused by the resignation, removal, or refusal to serve of the General Manager or trustees.

The Board shall annually elect an executive committee of five persons, who shall meet on the call of the General Manager and direct in the execution of orders and plans of the Board of Directors.

The Board of Directors shall make to the General Conference a report of its work, giving such facts in connection with the seminary as it may deem of importance.

General Manager.

4. The General Manager shall reside in Dayton,

Ohio, and shall manage the assets under the direction of the Executivē Committee, have charge of all the property, and manage the business of the institution. He shall solicit, and, by the consent and approval of the Board of Directors, or Executive Committee, employ others to solicit contributions to the seminary. In the name of the Union Biblical Seminary, and under its incorporate seal, the General Manager shall execute all deeds of transfer and other legal documents which may be authorized by the Board of Directors or its Executive Committee. He shall report to the Board of Directors annually, and to the General Conference, an account of all receipts and expenditures, and the general standing of the institution, with any other important facts or recommendations.

Support of the Seminary.

5. All moneys or values of any kind given to the seminary as an endowment shall be held sacred as a permanent fund and securely invested, the interest only to be used in the maintenance of the seminary. All other funds shall be used as the interests of the seminarv may require or as the donor may direct.

Annual Colleītions.

6. An equitable annual apportionment for the support of the seminary shall be made to the several annual conferences by the General Conference, or, under its direction, by the Board of Direct ors, and these sums shall be apportioned to the several charges, to be collected by the pastors, anu

9

reported to their respective conferences. Ten per cent of the funds thus secured may be used for the support of the libraries in the seminary.

Obligation of Faculty.

7. Each professor chosen to any chair in the seminary shall, upon the day of his inauguration, publicly subscribe to the following declaration of faith and obligation:

I solemnly declare, in the presence of God and the officers of Union Biblical Seminary, that I believe the Holy Scriptures, Old and New Testaments, to be the inspired word of God, and with the Holy Spirit, the only perfect rule of faith and practice. I believe in the confession of faith, as contained in the thirteen articles in our Book of Discipline, to be a truthful *consensus* of the fundamental doctrines of the Bible. I believe the system of church government, as presented in the Book of Discipline of the United Brethren in Christ, is consistent with the teachings of the Sacred Scriptures, and I solemnly promise that I will not teach or insinuate anything which shall in any way be inconsistent with this declaration or that which is not in harmony with the constitution and confession of faith and the rules of the Church as set forth in the Discipline of the United Brethren in Christ. I also promise, by divine assistance, to the best of my ability to sustain the doctrines of the Holy Scriptures as thus set forth by the Church in opposition to all forms of error, and this so long as I shall remain a professor in this institution.

(Name)————————————————————

V. SPECIAL EFFORT FOR EDUCATIONAL INSTITUTIONS.

In view of the urgent financial needs of the institutions of learning throughout the Church, the General Conference recommends that the quadrennium of 1889-1893 be devoted to a special effort on the part of the authorities and patrons to free these various institutions from debt, and secure them a complete endowment and equipment; and that the bishops give special aid to this endeavor by solicitation, public address, and writing. Agents of the respective institutions should confine themselves as much as possible to the bounds of their co-operating territories.

CHAPTER XXI.

HISTORICAL SOCIETY.

1. The Historical Society of the Church of the United Brethren in Christ, located at Dayton, Ohio, having for its object the collecting and preserving of papers, records, books, and other materials bearing upon the history of the Church, has the recognition of the General Conference.

2. Said society shall, through its officers, make quadrennial reports to the General Conference.

CHAPTER XXII.
BOUNDARIES.
SECTION I.
BISHOPS' DISTRICTS.

East Distrist.

Pennsylvania, East Pennsylvania, Maryland, East German, Virginia, Parkersburg, Allegheny, Erie, and Tennessee conferences.

Northwest Distrist.

Michigan, St. Joseph, Upper Wabash, Rock River, North Michigan, Wisconsin, Minnesota, Iowa, Des Moines, Elkhorn and Dakota, West Nebraska, and Colorado conferences.

Southwest Distrist.

Arkansas Valley, Neosho, Kansas, Northwest Kansas, Southern Missouri, Illinois, Lower Wabash, White River, Indiana, Central Illinois, and East Nebraska conferences.

Ohio Distrist.

Scioto, Sandusky, Miami, Auglaize, Ohio German, Ontario, North Ohio, East Ohio, Kentucky, and Central Ohio conferences.

Pacific Distrist.

California, Oregon, and Walla Walla conferences.*.

Foreign Missionary Distrist.

Sherbro Mission Distrist, West Africa; Germany Mission Distrist.

NOTE.—In the stationing of the bishops they were not confined to these distrists, except in the case of the Pacific Distrist, but were dirested to attend the conferences in rotation.—[EDITOR.

SECTION II.

ANNUAL CONFERENCES.

Allegheny.

Beginning at the south-west corner of Mercer County, Pennsylvania; thence along the southern line of Mercer and Venango counties to Clarion County; thence north along the eastern line of Venango County to Warren County; thence along the southern line of Warren, McKean, and Potter counties; thence north along the eastern line of Potter County; thence along the state line between New York and Pennsylvania to the northeast corner of Bradford County; thence south along the eastern line of Bradford, Sullivan, and Lycoming county-lines to the Susquehanna River; thence down the said river to the mouth of the Juniata River; thence up the Juniata River to the Tuscarora Mountains; thence south along the summit of the Tuscarora Mountains to the state line between Maryland and Pennsylvania; thence along the southern boundary of Pennsylvania to the south-west corner of the state; thence northward along the western line of Pennsylvania˙ to place of beginning.

Arkansas Valley.

Beginning at the northwest corner of Neosho Conference; thence west to Colorado line; thence south to the south˙ line of Oklahoma Territory; thence east along the south line of said territory to the west line of Neosho Conference; thence north to the place of beginning.

Auglaize.

Beginning at Union City, Indiana ; thence west with the Bellefontaine & Indianapolis Railroad, to Winchester ; thence on a straight line to the southeast corner of Huntington County, Indiana ; thence on the east line of said county north to the Wabash River ; thence down said river to the crossing of the Wabash, St. Louis & Pacific Railroad ; thence with said railroad to Ft. Wayne, including said city ; thence along the line of North Ohio Conference to Defiance ; thence along the line of Sandusky Conference to Cairo ; thence on a straight line to the northwest corner of Hardin County, Ohio ; thence east with the north line of said county ; thence south with the east line of said county to the southeast corner thereof ; thence on the north and east lines of Union County, to the Delaware and Springfield branch of the Cleveland, Columbus, Cincinnati & Indianapolis Railroad ; thence with said railroad to Milford Center, Ohio ; thence with the Pan-Handle Railroad including Urbana, Horatio, and Bradford ; thence northwest along the narrow-gauge railroad to Renville ; thence west on the Cleveland, Columbus, Cincinnati & Indianapolis Railroad to Union City, the place of beginning. The Waterhouse Chapel shall still be permitted to be served by the preacher in charge of Hill Grove Circuit, Miami Conference.

California.

Includes the State of California.

Central Illinois.

Beginning at Peru, on the Illinois River ; thence

up the Illinois River to the mouth of the Kankakee
River; thence with the Chicago Branch of the Illinois Central Railroad to Tolono; thence with the
Great Western Railway to Bement; thence direct
to Shelbyville; thence down the Okaw River to
Vandalia; thence direct to the mouth of the Illinois River; thence up said river to the place of
beginning.

Central Ohio.

Beginning at Zanesville, on the Muskingum
River; thence west on the Maysville pike to Lancaster; thence west on the Muskingum Valley
Railroad to the east boundary-line of Miami Conference (Pontius appointment remaining with Pickaway Circuit); thence north along the east lines of
Miami and Auglaize conferences to Forest, on the
Pittsburg, Fort Wayne, and Chicago Railroad;
thence east along said road to the east line of
Richland County, to Sandusky Conference (so as to
retain in Sandusky Conference, Forest, Pleasant
Ridge, Upper Sandusky, North Robinson, Crest-
line, and Osceola circuits); thence south to the
north-east corner of Knox County, along said
county line of Coshocton County to Dresden;
thence along Muskingum River to Zanesville, the
place of beginning.

Colorado

Bounded by the Union Pacific Railroad on the
north, and by the state lines of Colorado on the
east, south, and west.

Des Moines.

Embraces all that part of the State of Iowa west of the Iowa Conference line. .

East German Conference.

Beginning at the north-west corner of Bucks County, Pennsylvania; thence along the line of the East Pennsylvania Conference to the Susquehanna River; thence up said river to the south-west corner of Lycoming County; provided, that Snyder and Union counties and that part of Juniata County now occupied by the East German Conference remain in said conference; thence northward along the Allegheny Conference line to the north-east corner of Bradford County, Pennsylvania; thence east along the state line between New York and Pennsylvania to the Delaware River; thence down said river to the place of beginning; provided, that the ·First and Third churches in Baltimore remain in the East German Conference.

East Nebraska.

Embraces all that part of Nebraska south of Platte River and east of the West Nebraska Conference line.

East Ohio.

Embraces the following: Beginning at the north-east corner of the State of Ohio; thence south with the state line and Ohio River to Marietta; thence up the Muskingum River to Dresden, (embracing Hanover, opposite Marietta); thence west to the south-west corner of Coshocton County; thence directly north to the north-east corner of Knox County; thence west to the south-west corner of Ashland County; thence north to the mouth of Vermillion River; thence east along the shore of Lake Erie to the place of beginning; provided, that Orangeville Church in Ohio remain with Erie Conference, and Beaver Church in Pennsylvania with East Ohio Conference.

East Pennsylvania.

Beginning at the Atlantic Ocean; thence along the forty-first parallel of north latitude to the Delaware River; thence down said river to the north-east corner of Bucks County, Pennsylvania; thence along the north-west boundary line of said county to the Montgomery line; thence along the line between Montgomery and Lehigh counties to Berks County; thence along the line between Berks and Montgomery counties to the north-east corner of Douglas Township in Berks County; thence along the northern and western lines of Douglas Township, the northern line of Amity Township, and the northern and western lines of Exeter Township in Berks County to the Philadelphia and Reading Railroad; thence up said railroad to the upper depot of the city of Reading; provided, that the city of Reading be occupied in common by the East Pennsylvania and East German conferences; thence westward along the line of Lebanon Valley Railroad to the line between Lebanon and Dauphin counties; thence northward and eastward along said county line to the Schuylkill County line;

thence northward along said county line to the top
of Berry Mountain; thence along said mountain to
the Susquehanna River; thence down said river
and the Chesapeake Bay to the Atlantic Ocean;
thence northward along the Atlantic seacoast to
the place of beginning; provided, that the towns
of Avon and Palmyra remain in East German Conference, and Otterbein Church of Harrisburg in
Pennsylvania Conference.

Elkhorn and Dakota.

Commencing at the mouth of the Platte River;
north along the Iowa and Minnesota state lines to
the north-west corner of Pipestone County; thence
west to the west line of Dakota; thence south to
the north line of town twenty-four in Nebraska;
thence east on said line to the source of Cedar
River; thence down said river to Fullerton; thence
south to the Platte River; thence east along said
river to the place of beginning.

Erie.

Beginning at the shore of Lake Erie, at the
north-west corner of the State of Pennsylvania;
thence south along the state line between Ohio and
Pennsylvania to the south-west corner of Mercer
County, Pennsylvania; thence east with the line as
described in the bounding of the Allegheny Conference to the New York state line, and including
the State of New York and all that part of Pennsylvania embraced within the above described
limits.

Illinois.

Beginning at the junction of the Mississippi and Rock rivers; thence up the latter stream to the crossing of the Chicago, Rock Island & Pacific Railroad; thence east with said railroad to the Illinois River; thence down the Illinois River to its mouth; thence up the Mississippi to the place of beginning.

Indiana.

Beginning at the south-east corner of Franklin County, Indiana; thence along the line of the White River Conference, as described in the ` boundaries of that conference, to the White River due west of Franklin, Indiana; thence down said river, and the Wabash, to the Ohio River; thence up said river to the mouth of the Great Miami River; thence up the state line between Ohio and Indiana to the place of beginning.

Iowa.

Embraces all that part of the State of Iowa east of the following boundary line: Beginning at the north-west corner of Winnebago County; thence south to the south-west corner of Wright County; thence east to the north-west corner of Hardin County; thence south along the county line to the north line of Stony County; thence east to the north-east corner of Marshall County; thence south to the south-east corner of Jasper County; thence west to the south-west corner of Jasper County; thence south to the Chicago, Burlington & Quincy Railroad; thence west along said railroad to the west line of Lucas County; thence south to the state line.

Kansas.

Beginning at the south-east corner of Miami County, Kansas: thence west to the center of McPherson County: thence north to the Nebraska and Kansas line; thence east to the Missouri River; thence on the Kansas and Missouri line to the place of beginning.

Lower Wabash.

Beginning at Gosport, on White River; thence with the railroad to Greencastle; thence with the Indianapolis & Terre Haute Railroad, so as to include Knightstown and Terre Haute to the Wabash River; thence up said river to the mouth of Brulett's Creek; thence up said creek to Cherry Point; thence west on the line of the Indianapolis, Decatur & Springfield Railroad, to and including Tuscola; thence north by the Illinois Central Railroad to Tolono; thence with the described boundary of the Central Illinois Conference to the mouth of the Illinois River; thence down the Mississippi River to Cairo; thence up the Ohio, Wabash, and west branch of White River to the place of beginning.

Maryland.

Embraces all of the State of Maryland not included in Pennsylvania Conference.

Miami.

Beginning at the mouth of the Great Miami River; thence north on the line between Ohio and

Indiana to Union City, and to include that city; thence east with the Cleveland, Columbus, Cincinnati & Indianapolis·Railroad to Versailles; thence with the Toledo & Northern Narrow Gauge Railroad to Bedford; thence east with the Pittsburg, Cincinnati & St. Louis Railway to the east line of Champaign County, Ohio, including Piqua; thence south on the east line of the counties of Champaign, Green, Clinton, and a part of Brown County, to Ripley; thence down the Ohio River to the place of beginning.

Michigan.

Beginning at the shore of Lake Erie, at the northeast corner of Monroe County, Michigan; thence west, on the north line of Lenawee, Hillsdale, and Branch counties to the Grand Rapids & Indiana Railroad; thence by said railroad to Kalamazoo: thence by the South Haven & Kalamazoo Railroad to South Haven; thence along the shore of Lake Michigan to Grand Haven; thence by the Detroit & Milwaukee Railroad east to Detroit; thence down the Detroit River and the western shore of Lake Erie to the place of beginning.

Missouri.

Embraces all that part of the State of Missouri lying north of the Missouri River.

Minnesota.

Embraces all the State of Minnesota and the counties of Grant, Dual, and Codington, of Dakota.

Neosho.

Beginning at the south-west corner of Chautauqua County, Kansas; thence north to the south line of Kansas Conference; thence due east to the north-east corner of Linn County; thence south to the state line; thence south to the south-east corner of Indian Territory; thence west on territory line to a point south of the south-west corner of Chautauqua County, Kansas; thence north to the place of beginning.

North Michigan.

Embraces that part of the State of Michigan north of the Detroit, Milwaukee, and Grand Haven Railroad.

Northwest Kansas.

Beginning on the north at the center of Republic County; thence south to the north line of Arkansas Valley Conference; thence west to the Colorado line; thence north to the Nebraska line; thence east to the place of beginning, including the town of Concordia.

North Ohio.

Beginning at the north-west corner o. ʌranch County, Michigan; thence east on the north lines of Branch, Hillside, Lenawee, and Monroe counties, to the north-east corner of Monroe County; thence on the coast of Lake Erie to the mouth of Maumee River; thence up said river to Defiance, Ohio, leaving the city of Toledo to Sandusky Conference; thence up the Wabash, St. Louis, and Pacific Railroad, (the towns which this line touches to be included within North Ohio Conference) to Fort Wayne; thence (leaving Fort Wayne to Au-

glaize Conference) on the Fort Wayne and Chicago
Railroad to Columbia, Whitely County; thence due
north to the line of Noble County; thence east to
the corner of Noble County; thence north, including the Salem appointment within North Ohio
Conference, to the state line of Michigan; thence
west to the south-west corner of Branch County;
thence to the place of beginning.

Ohio German.

Bounded by the state lines of Ohio, Kentucky,
Indiana, and Illinois. They are permitted to go
into any of the Western states or territories, where
doors of usefulness open unto them, to labor among
the German population.

Ontario.

Includes all of the Province of Ontario, in the
Dominion of Canada.

Oregon.

Includes in its territory all that portion of country lying west of the Cascade range of mountains,
in both Oregon and Washington Territory.

Parkersburg.

Beginning on the summit of the Allegheny Mountains, at the line between Pennsylvania and Virginia; thence along the summit of said mountains
south-west to the line between Virginia and North
Carolina; thence west on said line to the south-west
corner of the State of Virginia; thence with the
Virginia and Kentucky line north to the Ohio
River; thence with said river to the Pennsylvania

state line; thence east on said line to the place of beginning.

Pennsylvania.

Beginning on the summit of South Mountain on the line between Maryland and Pennsylvania; thence to Westminister, Maryland; thence to Baltimore, including that city; thence along the Chesapeake Bay to the mouth of the Susquehanna River: thence up said river to the mouth of the Juniata River, except that Otterbein Church of Harrisburg and Deman's Island belong to Pennsylvania Conference; thence up the Juniata River to the Tuscarora Mountains; thence along the summit of said mountains to the line between Pennsylvania and Maryland; thence along said line to the place of beginning.

Rock River.

Beginning at the junction of the Mississippi and Rock rivers; thence east with the north boundary of the Illinois Central, Illinois, and Upper Wabash conferences to the Indiana state line; thence north on said line to Lake Michigan, around the border of Lake Michigan to the Wisconsin state line; thence along said state line to the Mississippi River; thence down said' river to the place of beginning.

Sandusky.

Beginning at the mouth of the Vermillion River, on Lake Erie; thence on an air-line south, to the south-west corner of Ashland County; thence with the north and west lines of Knox County, to the south-west corner of said county; thence to the north-west corner of Trenton Township, Delaware County; thence to the south-east corner of Genoa Township, of the same county; thence west on the Scioto Conference line, embracing Pleasant Valley, in Madison County; thence along the east and north lines of Union County, to the south-east corner of Hardin County; thence along the east and north lines of said county to the north-west corner thereof; thence on a straight line to Cairo; thence to Kalida; thence to Defiance; thence down the Maumee River, including all of the city of Toledo, and along the southern shore of Lake Erie to the place of beginning.

Scioto.

Beginning at Zanesville, on the Muskingum River; thence west on the Maysville pike to Lancaster; thence west on the Muskingum Valley Railroad to the east line of Miami Conference (Pontius appointment to remain on Pickaway Circuit); thence south, embracing Highland County and a part of Brown County, to Ripley, on the Ohio River; thence up said river to the mouth of Muskingum River; thence up said river to Zanesville, the place of beginning.

Southern Missouri.

Beginning at the south-west corner of the State of Missouri; thence running south along the line between Arkansas and Indian Territory to the south line of the fourth tier of counties in Ar-

10

kansas; thence east to the east line of the state;
thence north to Missouri state line; thence to the
mouth of the Missouri River; thence west with
said river to the state line; thence south to the
place of beginning.   ＼

St. Joseph.

Beginning at Peru, Indiana, on the Wabash
River; thence up said river to Huntington; thence
up the Auglaize Conference line to Ft. Wayne;
thence by the Pittsburg, Ft. Wayne & Chicago
Railroad, to Columbia City; thence due north to
the line of Noble County; thence east to the south-
east corner of said county; thence north on the
east lines of Noble and Lagrange counties to the
Michigan state line; thence west to the south-east
corner of St. Joseph County; thence on the east
and north lines of said county to the Grand Rapids
& Indiana Railroad; thence by said railroad to
Kalamazoo, Michigan; thence by the Kalamazoo
& South Haven Railroad to Lake Michigan; thence
along the lake shore to the line of Illinois and Indiana; thence south to Michigan City; thence by
the Lafayette & Michigan City Railroad to Lafayette, Indiana, Michigan City, and all towns on said
railroad to belong to St. Joseph Conference; thence
along the Strawtown Road, including the towns
of Jefferson and Frankfort, to Frankfort, Indiana;
thence northward along the Frankfort & Logansport Railroad to Wildcat River; thence up said
river to the west line of Howard County; thence
along the west and north lines of said county to

the Indianapolis & Peru Railroad; thence along
said railroad to Peru, Indiana, the place of beginning.

Tennessee.

Embraces all that part of the State of Tennessee
east of a due north and south line drawn through
Nashville, the capital of the state.

Upper Wabash.

Beginning at Gosport, on White River, to the
crossing of the Indianapolis & Peru Railroad;
thence on the Strawtown Road to Lafayette; thence
by way of Lafayette & Michigan City Railroad
to Michigan City; thence west to the Illinois and
Indiana state line to Kankakee City; thence south
along the Chicago branch of the Illinois Central
Railroad to Tuscola, and including Tolono; thence
east with the line of Lower Wabash Conference to
place of beginning, including the towns of Brazil
and Newburg

Virginia.

Beginning at the southeast corner of the State of
Virginia; thence along the western shore of the
Chesapeake Bay to Baltimore; thence to Westmin-
ster; thence to the summit of the South Mountain,
on the state line between Maryland and Pennsylvania; thence west on said line to the summit of
the Allegheny Mountains; thence south, along the
summit of said mountains, to the state line between
Virginia and North Carolina; thence east on said
line to place of beginning. The Virginia Conference shall also include all the appointments

embraced in the Allegheny and New Germany circuits, now occupied by the said conference within the limits of Parkersburg Conference.

Walla Walla.

Includes all that portion of Oregon and Washington Territory lying east of the Cascade Mountains, and also Idaho Territory.

West Nebraska.

Beginning at the north-east corner of Hamilton County; thence south to the Thayer County line; thence east six miles; thence south to Nebraska state line; thence west to the south-west corner of the State of Nebraska; thence north to the southwest corner of Elkhorn and Dakota Conference; thence east and south along the boundary of said conference to the place of beginning.

White River.

Beginning at the south-west corner of Marion County, Indiana; thence north to the north-west corner of said county; thence east to White River; thence up said river to the crossing of the Indianapolis and Peru Railroad; thence along said railroad to the Strawtown and Frankfort road; thence along said road to Frankfort, Indiana; thence north along the Frankfort and Logansport Railroad to the Wildcat River; thence up said river to the west line of Howard County, Indiana; thence along the west and north lines of said county to the Indianapolis and Peru Railroad; thence along said railroad to the Wabash River; thence up said

river to the Wells County line; thence south to the
south-east corner of Huntington County; thence
on a straight line to Winchester; thence eastward
along the railroad to the Ohio and Indiana state
line; thence south along the state line to the south-
east corner of Franklin County, Indiana; thence
westward to Greensburg; thence to Columbus;
thence to Nashville; thence west to White River;
thence up the river to the south line of Marion
County: thence west to the south-west corner of
said county.

Wisconsin.

Embraces all of the State of Wisconsin.

CHAPTER XXIII.

FORMULAS.

SECTION I.

ORDINATION OF ELDERS.

1. On the day appointed there shall be a suitable sermon delivered.

2. After their names have been read aloud, the
bishop or elder shall read the following articles to
all who may be chosen for ordination:

An elder "must be blameless, as the steward of
God; not self-willed, not soon angry, not given to
wine, no striker, not given to filthy lucre; but a
lover of hospitality, a lover of good men, sober,
just, holy, temperate; holding fast the faithful
word as he hath been taught, that he may be able
by sound doctrine both to exhort and to convince
the gainsayers." (Titus i: 7-9.)

Ques. Are you assured that you are inwardly moved by the Holy Ghost to take upon you the office of the ministry, to serve God in the church of Christ to the honor and glory of his holy name? If so, answer, " I trust I am."

Ques. Do you believe the Holy Scriptures, Old and New Testament? If so, answer, "I do believe them."

Ques. Will you apply due diligence to frame and fashion your life according to the doctrines of Christ, and to make yourself, as much as in you lieth, a wholesome example to the flock of Christ? If so, answer, "I will, the Lord being my helper."

Ques. Will you obey them to whom the charge and government over you is committed, and follow their godly admonitions with a willing and ready mind? If so, answer, "I will endeavor, through the grace of God, to do so."

Then prayer is to be offered.

After prayer, the bishop and elders shall lay their hands upon the head of each of them, and say:

Take thou authority to execute the office of an elder in the church of God, in the name of the Father, and of the Son, and of the Holy Ghost. Amen.

Hereupon the bishop or elder shall deliver to each of them the Holy Bible, saying:

Take thou authority to preach the word of God and administer the ordinances in the church of Christ.

Then the bishop or elder shall pray. And after prayer he shall read from Luke 12: 35-38:

"Let your loins be girded about, and your lights burning; and ye yourselves like unto men that wait for their lord, when he will return from the wedding; that when he cometh and knocketh, they may open unto him immediately. Blessed are those servants, whom the lord when he cometh shall find watching: verily I say unto you, that he shall gird himself, and make them to sit down to meat, and will come forth and serve them. And if he shall come in the second watch, or come in the third watch, and find them so, blessed are those servants."

After this, the following benediction is to be pronounced:

The peace of God keep your hearts and minds in the knowledge of Jesus Christ our Lord. Amen.

SECTION II.
MARRIAGE CEREMONY.

We are gathered together in the sight of God, and in the presence of these witnesses, to join together N. and M. as husband and wife. If any person present knows any just cause or impediment why these persons should not be joined in marriage, let the same now speak or forever after keep silent.

[If no impediment be alleged, then shall the minister say:]

Do you, and each of you, in the sight of God, and in the presence of these witnesses, covenant to live together after God's ordinance as husband

and wife, loving, honoring, and cherishing each
other in sickness and in health, in prosperity and
in adversity, forsaking all others and cleaving to
each other so long as you both shall live?   If so,
answer, "I do."   Join your right hands.

"Those whom God hath joined together, let no
man put asunder."

Inasmuch as you have consented together in
Christian marriage in the sight of God and in the
presence of these witnesses, I pronounce you husband and wife, in the name of the Father, Son,
and Holy Ghost.   Amen.

SECTION III.
BURIAL OF THE DEAD.

After the coffin is lowered into the grave, the
minister, if the deceased is a child or an adult
Christian, shall repeat the following:

"Man that is born of a woman is of few days,
and full of trouble.   He cometh forth like a flower,
and is cut down: he fleeth also as a shadow, and
continueth not."   "Lord, make me to know mine
end, and the measure of my days, what it is; that
I may know how frail I am."

In the midst of life we are in death; unto
whom should we seek for succor but unto thee, O
Lord, who for our sins art justly displeased?   Our
hope is in thy Son Jesus Christ, who hath said, "I
am the resurrection, and the life: he that believeth
in me, though he were dead, yet shall he live: and
whosoever liveth and believeth in me shall never
die."   "For we know that if our earthly house of

this tabernacle were dissolved, we have a building of God, a house not made with hands, eternal in the heavens."

"And I heard a voice from heaven saying unto me, Write, Blessed are the dead which die in the Lord from henceforth: Yea, saith the Spirit, that they may rest from their labours; and their works do follow them."

"There shall be no more death, neither sorrow, nor crying, neither shall there be any more pain: for the former things are passed away."

Inasmuch as God in his wise providence has called out of time into eternity the soul of our (brother, sister, or child,) we commit his (or her) remains to the ground, earth to earth, ashes to ashes, dust to dust, in the confident hope of the general resurrection through the Lord Jesus Christ, at his coming and glory; that this corruptible body shall be raised up and be fashioned like unto the glorious body of Christ, be reunited with the soul, and be received into everlasting habitations. Amen.

BENEDICTION.

SECTION IV.
CHURCH-DEDICATION SERVICE.

1. Scripture reading (Psalm 84; or, Isaiah 62 and Psalm 122.)

2. Singing.

3. Prayer.

4. Singing.

5. Sermon.

6. Monetary offering.

7. Singing.

8. Reading, with congregation standing :

But will God indeed dwell on the earth? behold, the heaven and heaven of heavens cannot contain thee; how much less this house that I have builded?

"Yet have thou respect unto the prayer of thy servant, and to his supplication, O Lord my God, to hearken unto the cry and to the prayer, which thy servant prayeth before thee to day :

"That thine eyes may be open toward this house night and day, even toward the place of which thou hast said, My name shall be there : that thou mayest hearken unto the prayer which thy servant shall make toward this place.

"And hearken thou to the supplication of thy servant, and of thy people Israel, when they shall pray toward this place : and hear thou in heaven thy dwelling place, and when thou hearest, forgive.

"If any man trespass against his neighbour, and an oath be laid upon him to cause him to swear, and the oath come before thine altar in this house: \ then hear thou in heaven, and do, and judge thy servants, condemning the wicked, to bring his way upon his head; and justifying the righteous, to give him according to his righteousness. `

."When thy people Israel be smitten down before the enemy, because they have sinned against thee, and shall turn again to thee, and confess thy name, and pray, and make supplication unto thee in this house: then hear thou in heaven, and forgive the sin of thy people Israel, and bring them again unto the land which thou gavest unto their fathers.

"When heaven is shut up, and there is no rain, because they have sinned against thee; if they pray toward this place, and confess thy name, and turn from their sin, when thou afflictest them: then hear thou in heaven, and forgive the sin of thy servants, and of thy people Israel, that thou teach them the good way wherein they should walk, and give rain upon thy land, which thou hast given to thy people for an inheritance.

"If there be in the land famine, if there be pestilence, blasting, mildew, locust, or if there be caterpillar; if their enemy besiege them in the land of their cities; whatsoever plague, whatsoever sickness there be; what prayer and supplication soever be made by any man, or by all thy people Israel, which shall know every man the plague of his own heart, and spread forth his hands toward this house: then hear thou in heaven thy dwelling place, and forgive, and do, and give to every man according to his ways, whose heart thou knowest; (for thou, even thou only, knowest the hearts of all the children of men;) that they may fear thee all the days that they live in the land which thou gavest unto our fathers.

"Moreover concerning a stranger, that is not of thy people Israel, but cometh out of a far country for thy name's sake; (for they shall hear of thy great name, and of thy strong hand, and of thy stretched out arm:) when he shall come and pray toward this house; hear thou in heaven thy dwelling place, and do according to all that the stranger calleth to thee for: that all people of the earth may know thy name, to fear thee, as do thy people Israel; and that they may know that this house, which I have builded, is called by thy name.' (I. Kings 8: 27-43.)

"We will go into his tabernacles: we will worship at his footstool." (Psalm 132: 7.)

"For the Lord hath chosen Zion; he hath desired it for his habitation.

"This is my rest for ever: here will I dwell; for I have desired it.

"I will abundantly bless her provision: I will satisfy her poor with bread. I will also clothe her priests with salvation: and her saints shall shout aloud for joy." (Psalm 132: 13-16.)

"Now, my God, let, I beseech thee, thine eyes be open, and let thine ears be attent unto the prayer that is made in this place.

"Now therefore arise, O Lord God, into thy resting place, thou, and the ark of thy strength: let thy priests, O Lord God, be clothed with salvation, and let thy saints rejoice in goodness." (II. Chron. 6: 40, 41.)

"Blessed be the Lord God of Israel from everlasting to everlasting, and let all the people say, Amen. Praise ye the Lord." (Psalm 106: 48.)

9. Charge to the trustees.

10. Delivery of the keys in the name of the Trinity to hold in trust for God and the United Brethren in Christ.

11. Doxology.

12. Benediction.

FORMS.

TRANSFERS.

Form of Transfer of Preacher.

This is to certify that —— is a regular ——
of the Church of the United Brethren in Christ,
of —— Conference, and is hereby transferred
to ——Conference of said church.

[Date, etc.]

Form of Certificate of Transfer of Member.

This is to certify that A. B. is an acceptable member of the United Brethren in Christ, at —— Class,
————Charge, —— Conference, and is hereby
transfefred to ——Society, of ——Charge, ——
Conference.

....Pastor.

[Date, etc.]

Form of Certificate of Membership.

This is to certify that A. B. is a member in good
standing of the Church of the United Brethren in
Christ at ————, and is hereby recommended to
the confidence and fellowship of Christians everywhere.

....Pastor.

[Date, etc.]

158 DISCIPLINE.

Form of Certificate of Dismissal.

This is to certify that A. B. has been until this date a member in good standing in the Church of the United Brethren in Christ, at ——, and at —— request is dismissed from the Church by a vote of the class.

..................................Pastor.
[Date, etc.]

————

BEQUESTS.

HOME, FRONTIER, AND FOREIGN MISSIONARY SOCIETY.

I give and bequeath to the Home, Frontier, and Foreign Missionary Society of the United Brethren in Christ, organized by the General Conference of said church, May 20, 1853, and incorporated in Butler County, Ohio, September 23, 1854, the sum of —— dollars; and the receipt of the treasurer of the society shall be a sufficient discharge thereof to my executors and administrators.

————

WOMAN'S MISSIONARY ASSOCIATION.

I give, devise, and bequeath to the Woman's Missionary Association of the United Brethren in Christ, for........................   ....Dollars.

REPORTS.

FORM OF PREACHER'S REPORT.

Quarterly Report, —— *Annual Conference,*
United Brethren in Christ.

	Classes or Fields of Labor.

...............District. ....Circuit. ....Mission. ....Quarter. ....188...	Salem....	Bethel....	Shiloh....	Union....	Liberty...	Zion....	Fairview.	Carmel...	&c	Totals....
Members received.........										
Members lost...............										
Members at present.......										
Baptisms.....................										
Discourses preached......										
Pastoral visits.............										
Class-meetings held.......										
Preacher's salary...........										
Presiding elder's salary..										
Telescopes...................										
Children's Friends.........										
Missionary Visitors.......										
For the Little Ones.......										
Quarterlies..................										
Scholars in S. S............										
Collected for missions...										
Collected for local S. S..										
Col. for church expenses										
Collected for...............										
Collected for...............										
Collected for...............										
Collected for...............										

....Name.

[The blanks can be filled out to suit either pastor or
presiding elder, as the presiding elder would simply give
the total column of each work.]

SABBATH-SCHOOL SUPERINTENDENT'S REPORT.

.... *Sabbath-school*, ... *Quarter.*

....(Date).

1. Number of officers and teachers...................

2. Number of scholars enrolled........................

3. Average attendance.................................

4. Children's Friends.................................

5. Missionary Visitors................................

6. Lessons for the Little Ones........................

7. Quarterlies ....

8. Bible Teachers....................................

9. Amount of collections.............................

10. Expenses of the quarter..........................

11. Missions...

Remarks.

..............................Superintendent.

CLASS LEADER'S REPORT.

.... *Class,* .... *Quarter.*

.................................(*Date.*)

1. Number of members...............................

2. Number of meetings held ....

3. Average attendance..............................

CONTRIBUTION CARD.

.... *Church,* ....(*Date.*)

I hereby agree to pay to the order of the treasurer of .... Church the sum of ....,
weekly, during the year commencing ....,
for pastor's salary and other church expenses.

(Signature)................................

INDEX.

11   161

Bishops—Annual meeting of, 62; announcement of repre-
sentation in General Conference by, 45; attendance at
conference, 61; delinquency of, 63; duties of, 18, 61;
election of, 18, 60; eligibility to office of, 18; *emeritus*,
60; *pro tem*, 43; residence of, 60; salaries of, 61; stationing of, 60; vacancy in office of, 63.

Board of Education, 121. (See Education, Board of.)

Boundaries, 132; bishops' districts, 132; annual conferences, 133.

Book Committee, 93.

Branch missionary societies, 105; contributions to, 106;
secretary of, 106; treasurer of, 106.

Branch Society, W. M. A., Constitution of, 111.

Building of church-houses and parsonages, 86.

Burial of dead, 152.

CALIFORNIA Conference, Boundary of, 134.

Central Illinois Conference, Boundary of, 134.

Central Ohio Conference, Boundary of, 135.

Certificate of dismissal, 158; of membership, 157.

Charters, 93.

Church-Erection Society, 114.

Church-houses, 85; trustees of, 85; building of, 86;
vacant, 87; dedication of, 153.

Church records, 73.

Circulation of Church literature, duty regarding, 73.

Classes, 34; appointments to, 34; division of, 34; dis-
banding of, 34.

Classification of ministry, 55; how determined, 56.

Class leaders, Dismissal of, 35; duties of, 26, 35, 37; in
elections to General Conference, 46; in trials, 30;
election of, 34; qualifications, 35; records of, 32

Class stewards, appointment of, 35; dismissal of, 36;
duties, 36; in elections to General Conference, 46.

Collections, General, 74; missionary, 62, 74.

Colleges, 126.

Colorado Conference, Boundary of, 135.

www.ingramcontent.com/pod-product-compliance
Lightning Source LLC
Chambersburg PA
CBHW030849270326
41928CB00008B/1289